M000215182

A CHRISTIAN GUIDE TO
ENVIRONMENTAL ISSUES

The Bible Reading Fellowship
15 The Chambers, Vineyard
Abingdon OX14 3FE
brf.org.uk

The Bible Reading Fellowship (BRF) is a Registered Charity (233280)

ISBN 978 1 80039 005 8
First published 2015
This revised edition published 2021
All rights reserved

Text © Martin J. Hodson and Margot R. Hodson 2021
This edition © The Bible Reading Fellowship 2021
Cover photos: *front, clockwise from top left*, 1, Martin Hodson; 2, 3, 6, Elizabeth
Perry; 4, benjaminnolte/stock.adobe.com; 5, Alto Crew from Unsplash; *back*, soil,
Martin Hodson; women sewing, Elizabeth Perry

The authors assert the moral right to be identified as the authors of this work

Acknowledgements
Unless otherwise stated, scripture quotations are taken from The Holy Bible, New
International Version (Anglicised edition) copyright © 1979, 1984, 2011 by Biblica.
Used by permission of Hodder & Stoughton Publishers, an Hachette UK company.
All rights reserved. 'NIV' is a registered trademark of Biblica. UK trademark number
1448790.

Every effort has been made to trace and contact copyright owners for material
used in this resource. We apologise for any inadvertent omissions or errors, and
would ask those concerned to contact us so that full acknowledgement can be
made in the future.

A catalogue record for this book is available from the British Library

MARTIN J. HODSON &
MARGOT R. HODSON

A CHRISTIAN GUIDE TO
ENVIRONMENTAL
ISSUES

Photocopying for churches

Please report to CLA Church Licence any photocopy you make from this publication. Your church administrator or secretary will know who manages your CLA Church Licence.

The information you need to provide to your CLA Church Licence administrator is as follows:

Title, Author, Publisher and ISBN

If your church doesn't hold a CLA Church Licence, information about obtaining one can be found at **uk.ccli.com**

ACKNOWLEDGEMENTS

We are very grateful to Olivia Warburton, Daniele Och and the staff at The Bible Reading Fellowship for their patience and advice during the publication process.

A number of our friends and colleagues wrote us short stories which really added to the book: Barbara Brighouse, Marcial Felgueiras, Steve Hughes, Kailean Khongsai, Andy Lester, Caroline Pomeroy, Dr Andrew Rosenthal, John Sibley, Dr Robert Sluka, Chris Stapleton, Helen Stephens, Richard Thornbury and Rob Walrond.

The following advised us on various aspects of the book: Dr John McKeown, Dr Elizabeth Perry and Dr Chris Walley. Thanks also to Elizabeth for providing some of the cover photographs.

The first edition of this book was written while we were on sabbatical leave in 2014, and we are grateful to The John Ray Initiative, the Diocese of Oxford and Haddenham Benefice (now Wychert Vale Benefice) for allowing us this time to think and write. We worked on the second edition during summer 2020 and amid the Covid-19 pandemic. We would like to thank all those who encouraged us during that summer.

A Rocha UK supported this project throughout, and we are grateful for all their helpful suggestions and advice.

This book is dedicated to the memory of our parents,
Donald and Ethel Hodson and Jim and Doreen Perry,
who raised us to love and respect the natural world.

We would also like to dedicate this second edition
to the memory of Sir John Houghton and Professor Sam Berry,
who founded The John Ray Initiative and inspired us in our work
of environmental education in the church.

CONTENTS

ABBREVIATIONS

AIDS	acquired immune deficiency syndrome
BBC	British Broadcasting Corporation
CCIH	Christian Connections for International Health
CCS	carbon capture and storage
CED	Christian Engineers in Development
CMS	Church Mission Society
CO_2	carbon dioxide
COP 15, 21, 26	Conference of the Parties 15, 21, 26
Covid-19	'Corona Virus Disease 2019' is the name given to the illness caused by SARS-CoV-2. This was to avoid confusion with SARS-CoV-1 and to avoid geographical locations, animal species or people groups in the name.
DDT	dichlorodiphenyltrichloroethane
EIA	environmental impact assessment
EROEI	Energy Returned on Energy Invested
GDP	gross domestic product
GM	genetically modified
HIPPO	habitat destruction, invasive species, pollution, human overpopulation, and overharvesting
HLPE	High-Level Panel of Experts on Food Security and Nutrition

IAASTD	International assessment of agricultural knowledge, science and technology for development
IPCC	Intergovernmental Panel on Climate Change
JRI	The John Ray Initiative
MDG	Millennium Development Goal
MPA	Marine Protected Area
NASA	National Aeronautics and Space Administration
NGO	non-governmental organisation
ppm	parts per million
SARS-CoV-1	severe acute respiratory syndrome coronavirus (identified in April 2003 as the cause of the SARS epidemic in Asia that year)
SARS-CoV-2	severe acute respiratory syndrome coronavirus 2 (name adopted by the International Committee on Taxonomy of Viruses in February 2020 for the coronavirus responsible for the 2020 pandemic)
SDG	Sustainable Development Goal
SJI	Share Jesus International
TEEB	The Economics of Ecosystems and Biodiversity
UN	United Nations
UNFCCC	United Nations Framework Convention on Climate Change
USDA	United States Department of Agriculture
WWF	World Wide Fund for Nature

FOREWORD

'Is there hope?' is a question I am often asked. No doubt, the trends in biodiversity loss, climate change, plastics pollution and many other 'environmental' issues are very concerning, not to say potentially catastrophic. But, yes, there is hope. Not just ultimately, in a loving, creator God, but in him now.

One area that gives me hope is that more and more people, and whole sectors of society, are fast waking up to the reality of the environmental crisis. They want to act themselves, and they want governments to act, too. Churches and Christians are one such sector. In my five years as chief executive of A Rocha UK, I have witnessed an extraordinary awakening, as evidenced, for example, by the rocketing number of local churches, whole denominations and networks joining our Eco Church programme.

Churches and Christians are still present in every village, town and city neighbourhood in the UK. However stretched we may feel, we have a unique potential to make a positive impact on the environmental crisis locally and nationally if we act together, drawing on the Bible, science and the resources we do have.

Where there is little action, I find it is rarely because of a lack of concern, but rather due to a lack of confidence about where to start, what will make a real difference or how this fits with church mission and personal discipleship.

Margot and Martin's engaging book is a great place to start to build confidence, as well as a timely refresher for seasoned 'creation carers'. It combines practical theology and the latest science with years of experience teaching and living care for the environment. Reading it will provide any individual, home group or church with a solid foundation for effective action for all of God's creation in the critical decade ahead.

Read it and pass it on!

Andy Atkins, chief executive, A Rocha UK

PREFACE TO THE SECOND EDITION

The first edition of this book was written while on sabbatical in Spain during autumn 2014. By January 2020 it had become a popular book for those who wanted to understand environmental issues from a Christian perspective, and we were excited when BRF asked us to produce a second edition. Little did we realise that we were about to head into the Covid-19 lockdown and that the world would begin to change around us. Amid the sadness and demands of that time, our vicarage home became a new place of writing, and being at home enabled us to stand back once more and view the world from a fresh perspective.

We discuss the Covid-19 pandemic and other new human diseases of wild-animal origin in chapter 2, 'Biodiversity'. It is one of several environmental issues where there has been considerable change since 2014, and we have updated all the environmental sections to reflect the current situation and the latest evidence. There has been substantial change in the global political response to the environmental crisis and we reflect on that and on new grassroots movements, such as the school strikes for climate.

One of the most encouraging developments has been the growth of interest in the environment from Christians. This has been particularly marked in the UK, but has also grown in other European countries, in the global south and in many other parts of the world. The commitment of many denominations to see care for God's creation as a core part of our discipleship is very encouraging.

As we have been 'locked down' and writing this book during a time of global crisis, we have been most deeply aware that the threat of uncontrollable climate change is an even greater danger to the stability of society and the well-being of people and the world's biodiversity. We pray that out of this crisis, global leaders will learn the need to respect and care for the natural world. We hope that our work, along with the voices of many others, will play a small part in resourcing Christians to play an effective role as disciples of Christ in this century of environmental challenge.

Margot and Martin Hodson, February 2021

PROLOGUE:
LET THE TREES CLAP THEIR HANDS

In 2014 we were on study leave in Spain and Portugal, exploring environmental issues and writing the first edition of this book. For much of the time we were in a small apartment in the Alpujarra Mountains of Andalucía. On one day we walked up the beautiful valley of Pampaneira, Bubion and Capileira. We descended through pastures and into the deep valley, before walking through a chestnut forest. As we entered the wood, the wind came up and blew through the leaves of the trees. For a moment we were transported back to a city concert hall and the applause at the end of a performance. As the applause died away in our minds, the trees continued. They were clapping their hands! Further on, another voice took up the applause as we came across a mountain stream bubbling away and also praising its creator. Isaiah 55:12 describes how the trees of the field will clap their hands and in Psalm 98:8 the psalmist writes of rivers clapping their hands. As we explain the issues affecting the planet and our responsibility to respond, we hope we can provide some guidelines that will help us release the Earth to clap its hands.

DISCOVERING GOD'S EARTH

Starting the journey

Let's take a ferry to Spain! We'd been planning some extra leave for years. Martin had had a sabbatical in the past, but I (Margot) had never quite managed it. In the midst of very busy lives, we were longing to have a few weeks out from regular work to think, write and pray. We hoped to be able to stand back and gain a fresh perspective on all that we were doing. Our aims were to see what was happening to the environment in another part of Europe, visit some nature reserves and meet up with Christians and others who are concerned for the natural world. As supporters of A Rocha, a Christian environmental organisation, we regularly visit A Rocha UK in Southall and we especially wanted to return to A Rocha Portugal. We didn't want to fly, so the idea came to take the ferry. We packed a box of all those books that we had bought but never had time to read, gathered things for the journey and headed off to Portsmouth for the crossing to Santander in northern Spain.

Our focus for the trip was to write about the key environmental issues of today. What are the most urgent and what can we do about them? How do we understand them in the light of the Christian faith? For both of us, our concern for nature began when we were teenagers and we both came to a committed Christian faith as young adults. Martin became a Christian in Jerusalem when he had a research contract in the Botany Department of the Hebrew University. He later moved to Oxford and was a founding member of 'Sage', Oxford's Christian environmental group. My faith and green interests were forged together in the 'Geography Christian Fellowship' of Bristol University. We were a small group of geography students who met once a week to try to understand the human and natural world from a Christian perspective. It was in this group that I discovered how human society, nature and faith all fitted together. At the very heart of everything is a God of love.

As the ferry slid out of Portsmouth harbour, we looked at the horizon and were aware of the vastness of the planet and the enormity of the issues that are spread across it. Humans have had an impact on our world from the depths of the oceans to the upper atmosphere. There is nowhere on Earth that has escaped traces of human activity.

The state of our planet

Lots of people worry about the environment. Whether it is your local community beset by traffic fumes or building on green spaces, or wider concerns about the rainforests and climate change, lots of us have a feeling inside that things just are not the way they should be. So what is really going on?

In 2012, government representatives from around the world gathered in Rio de Janeiro in Brazil for 'Rio+20', where they were assessing progress, or lack of it, since the Rio Earth Summit of 1992. Back in the UK, I (Martin) was asked by A Rocha UK and Tearfund to design a 15-minute talk that would cover all of the world's environmental problems. This would form part of a 'Whose Earth?' Rio+20 presentation that would be given at a number of venues in England in summer 2012. To say something meaningful about all of our environmental problems in 15 minutes seemed a tall order. I needed to start somewhere, and I chose a picture of our planet. Then, while the opening talk was going on, the problems streamed in across the picture. My list is in the second column of table 1 below. I am far from the only person who has attempted a list of environmental problems. The American scientist Jared Diamond listed some key issues in his book *Collapse*[1] and these are shown in column 3. Finally, there has been much interest in 'planetary boundaries',[2] and these are shown in column 4. If we cross these biophysical thresholds it could have disastrous consequences for humanity.

Table 1   Environmental issues

Chapter of this book	Martin's list[a]	Diamond's list[b]	Planetary boundaries[c]
2 Biodiversity	Biodiversity loss		Changes in biosphere integrity
	Habitat loss	Destruction of natural habitats	Land-system change
		Overfishing	
		Loss of genetic diversity Alien (non-native) species	
3 Climate change	Climate change	Climate change	Climate change
4 Water	Water	Fresh water availability	Freshwater use
5 Human population and consumption	Human population	Human population growth	
	Consumption	Overconsumption	
6 Energy	Peak oil	Decreased supplies of fossil fuels	
7 Soil	Soil erosion	Soil erosion	
8 Food	Food supply		
9 Environment and sustainable development			
Covered in several chapters	Pollution	Toxic chemicals	Introduction of novel entities
	Political/social instability		

Not covered		Sunlight availability and a ceiling on photosynthetic capacity	
	Ocean acidification		Ocean acidification
			Biogeochemical flows
	Ozone depletion	Ozone hole	Stratospheric ozone depletion
			Atmospheric aerosol loading
	Acid rain		

a   A list of environmental problems put together by Martin for the 'Whose Earth?' presentations in 2012.

b   From Diamond, *Collapse*, chapter 16, pp. 486–95.

c   From Steffen et al. in *Science* (2015).

It can be seen immediately that different people, coming from different perspectives, come up with rather different lists. Sometimes people have subdivided problems, or lumped them together. So Diamond lists destruction of natural habitats, overfishing, loss of genetic diversity, and alien (non-native) species, which I covered in just two topics, biodiversity loss and habitat loss; these two are also listed as planetary boundaries (changes in biosphere integrity and land-system change). Whichever list you take, though, it all seems fairly daunting. We should also remember that these issues interact with each other in myriad ways, so keeping them in separate 'boxes' is never a good idea.

In a book like this one, we cannot possibly cover everything, so what will we look at? Quite evidently we need to cover biodiversity loss (chapter 2), and we will consider habitat loss there too, as it is a key driver of biodiversity loss. Everyone is in agreement that climate change (chapter 3) and water (chapter 4) need to be included. Human population (chapter 5) is, in many respects, a driver of other problems, and human (over)consumption is very much a linked topic. These first four topics are often seen as the 'big four' problems.

Energy (chapter 6), or how we power our society, has always been an important issue. Although we now have fewer worries over peak oil and decreased supplies of fossil fuels, the rapid global expansion of renewable energy, and concepts such as stranded assets and divestment from fossil fuels, make this an important subject to include. One topic that often seems to be neglected is soil (chapter 7). The problem is not just about soil erosion: soil is the basis for almost all of our agriculture and needs more attention. Food (chapter 8) is perhaps not truly an 'environmental issue', but it is affected by almost all of the other issues in some way, and is a very important topic for humanity.

The one issue that is not mentioned in any of our lists is environment and sustainable development (chapter 9). It is the world's poorest people who suffer most from environmental problems, and we feel that our book would not be complete without a chapter covering the balance between environment and sustainable development. We decided not to give a separate chapter to pollution, but examples occur in several chapters. The 'novel entities' planetary boundary includes chemical pollutants, microplastics and genetically modified organisms. Political and social instability was an issue mentioned only by me, in the 'Whose Earth?' presentation; it is definitely not an environmental issue but is frequently caused by these issues, at least in part.

Then there are a number of issues that we have decided to leave out. We do not wish to imply lack of importance, but space is limited. Diamond included 'sunlight availability and a ceiling on photosynthetic capacity' in his list, suggesting that this could limit agricultural productivity. This idea is controversial and is not now seen as very likely to be important.[3] Ocean acidification is a topic related to climate change as both are (largely) caused by atmospheric carbon dioxide. In the case of the oceans, the carbon dioxide dissolves in the water, making a dilute carbonic acid solution and increasing the acidity. This has the effect of making it more difficult for organisms such as coral, plankton and sea urchins to make their calcium carbonate shells. Biogeochemical flows include the nitrogen and phosphorus cycles, which are being seriously perturbed mainly by our overuse of inorganic fertilisers. We decided not to cover some planetary boundaries, at least partly because they are complex issues requiring a fair amount of knowledge of chemistry. They have been well covered by Mark Lynas in his book *The God Species*.[4] We spent some time looking at acid rain as a case study in a previous book.[5] This is, in some ways, related to the atmospheric aerosol loading boundary.

Looking at the whole of table 1, sadly we have to say that in only two cases do we have much of a handle on the problems: acid rain and ozone depletion. On both of these issues, world governments have taken action and the problems, if not solved, are at least under some control. All of the other problems are far from in hand.

As we were on sabbatical in Spain and Portugal, we took the opportunity to investigate some of the environmental issues and problems in those countries. In the following chapters we will include some of our findings.

Orca

Lists of environmental problems can get a bit depressing. It is always good to balance the problems by looking at something positive. On our ferry journey to Spain, we were delighted to find a wildlife charity called Orca on board. Orca uses ferry crossings to conduct wildlife research on cetaceans (whales, dolphins and porpoises).[6] Because ferries travel at the same times and speeds on the same routes through the year, they make ideal platforms from which to observe wildlife. In season, Brittany Ferries gives passage to two Orca wildlife guides on their crossings from England to Spain, who spend the trip scanning the horizon and recording all sightings of cetaceans. They are building up systematic data on these animals for the first time in the Bay of Biscay and have shown that there are higher populations than were previously thought, with 31 species of cetaceans in the European Atlantic.

Sadly, these animals, like many others, are under threat from the activities of humans. Fishing gear and propellers are both hazards. Plastic is a major problem for ocean species, and David Attenborough's *Blue Planet II* series had a worldwide impact in reducing single-use plastic. Some of that advance has been lost during the Covid-19 pandemic, through understandable medical uses and increased packaging with a rise of internet shopping. The impact of this is already being seen in the oceans. It is frightening to realise that plastic and other rubbish has been found at depths of 4,500 metres in European waters.[7] Humans have even left rubbish on the moon!

God's love for the natural world

Very often we read the Bible with questions about ourselves and the human world around us. This means that we sometimes skim over passages about the natural world, or even blank them out. God's creation is assumed to be a kind of wallpaper, his real interest being people.

There is a different approach. If you read the Bible looking for nature, you will find God's love for his creation at every twist and turn of the biblical drama. Things start in Genesis with the creation of the universe. As God forms each part of his creation, he declares it to be 'good'. We find wild and domestic animals being given a place in the ark. God makes sure that every species is able to survive the downpour.

God's love does not stop at animals. He also sees plants as 'good' and two trees in the story of Eden are shown to have special significance: the tree of life and the tree of the knowledge of good and evil. The resurrection of Jesus takes place in a garden and the tree of life reappears at the end of Revelation (see chapter 4). There is an unusual passage in Deuteronomy (20:19), which contains instructions about conducting a siege. It says that you should not cut down the fruit trees around the city because you can eat their fruit: 'Are the trees of the field people, that you should besiege them?' One of the sad truths about the environmental destruction that is happening today is that we are destroying our very means of survival. Humans will suffer the consequences alongside the rest of nature.

Care for creation is central to the Christian faith

Looking at the Bible with fresh eyes is both exciting and scary. It is exciting because new vistas are opened up and we find we understand things in new ways. It is scary because this discovery can be very challenging. We realise that the complacent way we have been living may need some re-examination. It raises questions about how God wants us to live as individuals and as churches. When I (Margot) was a student, the book *Rich Christians in an Age of Hunger* was relatively new.[8] It was hotly discussed in our Geography Christian Fellowship and led a generation of Christians in the west to face the reality of world poverty and our obligation to respond to it.

The biblical reflections in this book aim to explain just how central a concern for the environment has become and how urgent the need is to respond. We aim to provide a Christian perspective on each of the environmental themes, by exploring the environmental dimension to key ideas in Christian understanding. These build together to provide a biblical basis for Christian action. Our central theme is 'covenant', which runs through the book. At the end of this chapter, we offer a Bible study on 'Love and the greatest commandment'. This goes to the heart of the Christian faith and is a suitable starting point. Many writers have looked at the Genesis creation passages,[9] so chapter 2 considers the related theme of intrinsic value in the light of creation. This is linked to biodiversity and challenges the way we value the living world. The core idea of 'covenant' is the focus of the reflection in chapter 3, where we look at this with regard to climate change. If our relationship with the Earth is one of covenant, then our response to climate change is a spiritual issue and one that Christians need to address urgently. Covenant leads on to salvation, which is paired with water in chapter 4, because many of the salvation images in the Bible use water.

As we consider population and consumption in chapter 5, so we look at the twin issues of God's sovereignty and human responsibility. How much are we responsible for changing our lifestyles? Where is God's sovereignty in the population debate? These themes interact with the concept of sabbath, a subject that links with energy in chapter 6. In a 24/7 society, can the principle of sabbath help us to reassess our priorities? In the Hebrew Bible, breaking the covenant led to exile, and this in turn motivated God's people to return to him and his promise of salvation. Exile is the biblical theme in chapter 7, as we consider not only the serious implications of soil degradation worldwide but also the potential for the world when soil is managed well.

A crucial environmental truth of the Christian faith is that Jesus was physically born among us and resurrected in a physical (bodily) form. Both these key teachings affirm the material world and challenge us to engage with it. These concepts are explored in the light of food in chapter 8 and environment and sustainable development in chapter 9. We consider justice as we look at the disparity between the wealthy west and the greater poverty in the majority world. Early Christians were characterised by hope, and this is the theme of our final chapter as we draw everything together and point a way forward.

Alongside the Christian themes, we have stories and examples from many parts of the world. Some of these are from organisations that we have supported as we have made the journey of discovery on how to care for God's fragile world. We have asked some of our friends and colleagues to write short pieces on their work, and we are very grateful to them.

Introducing A Rocha and The John Ray Initiative

In 1983, Peter and Miranda Harris left their home in England to be mission partners with Crosslinks in southern Portugal. Peter and Miranda had a lifelong love for wildlife and felt called to find a way to conserve nature as part of their mission for the church. They set up a small field centre in the Alvor estuary in the Algarve and named their work 'A Rocha', which is Portuguese for 'The Rock'.[10] They developed a bird observatory and began to build up vital scientific data on the biodiversity of the Alvor peninsular. On our sabbatical trip we visited this centre once more (see chapter 10).

For many years, A Rocha's work was confined to Portugal, but then people who had been to the centre in Portugal started gradually to catch the vision, and other centres were established. It was not until 2001 that A Rocha UK[11] was founded by Dave Bookless in Southall, a very multicultural part of west London. A Rocha UK was involved in a large project to reclaim an area of west London heathland and turn it into a country park. They run the Wild Christian programme and the Eco Church scheme, and have several associated Partners in Action. Margot is on the board of A Rocha UK as the link person between them and The John Ray Initiative. Tragically, Peter and Miranda were involved in a major car crash in South Africa on 29 October 2019. Miranda was killed and Peter was seriously injured. Chris Naylor, the executive director of A Rocha International, and his wife Susanna were also killed in the crash. Our hearts go out to their families and the A Rocha family after this terrible event.

It is now over 35 years since the Harrises first stepped out to start an environmental centre as Christian mission. A Rocha currently has active ministry in many nations around the world. They have helped Christians grasp the need to understand nature as something that has value in its own right because it is created by God and valued by him. A Rocha put an emphasis on community, and they teach and live out a sustainable Christian lifestyle that is built on simplicity and a respect for all that God has created. We will look in more detail at some of the aspects of A Rocha's work around the world in later chapters.

The John Ray Initiative (JRI)[12] was founded in 1998 by Sir John Houghton and other senior scientists who were concerned at the scale of the environmental crisis and wished to give a Christian response. JRI has concentrated on education: running courses; putting on conferences and publishing papers and books. Margot is the director of theology and education for JRI and Martin has been their operations director since April 2009, running the small staff team. A Rocha UK and JRI have different strengths and often collaborate on projects.

All creation worships God

One of our favourite Psalms is 148, where each part of creation is called to worship God. Worship indicates relationship and, if God calls creation to worship, then he must have a relationship with the stars, sea creatures, fruit trees and wild animals. As we begin to consider our relationship with creation, we start with the wonderful understanding that God loves his creation, rejoices at its worship and has relationships with parts of it that we can only dream of.

 How environmentally friendly is your worship? You might like to look at some of the practical things at your church, such as single-use service sheets and the cups used for church coffee or Communion. Are things better or worse than before the pandemic? You could also think about the content of worship: the songs, prayers and teaching. How can we worship God in a way that respects his wonderful creation more fully?

Bible study: the greatest commandment

If you were given a Post-it note and asked to write down the most important thing to you, what would you write? In Jesus' day, asking for summaries of the law was common. With the whole of the biblical text to work through, what was the most important message? A popular tool for Bible study was to combine two texts that had a common word, to bring out a special insight. Jesus uses this tool to combine two verses that have the common word 'love'. We will now explore this passage.

Read Matthew 22:34–40

1 Jesus ranks his commandments: how can the second be derived from the first?
2 Can you think of examples of teaching in the Bible that hang on these two commandments?
3 What principles in your church derive from these two commandments?
4 How do we 'love God' in the light of our environmental crisis?
5 How do we 'love our neighbour'?

Read Luke 10:25–37

The parable of the good Samaritan is one of the most famous passages in the Bible. It is a fantastic story and has inspired Christians down through the ages. Jesus told the parable in response to the question, 'Who is my neighbour?' When we look at the environmental crisis today, we can ask that question afresh.

6 Should we consider 'our neighbour' to include the creatures of this world alongside humans?
7 Does that make any practical difference to our action to care for the environment?

Summary

These passages go to the heart of our motivation and standards for worship, relationships and ethical living. As we start to consider how we should live as Christians in a fragile world, we can look again at how we love God and love our neighbour. Taking a fresh look will influence our worship, relationships and the way we live.

Notes

1   J.M. Diamond, *Collapse: How societies choose to fail or succeed* (Penguin, 2005).
2   W. Steffen et al., 'Planetary boundaries: Guiding human development on a changing planet' *Science* 347, no. 6223 (2015), **science.sciencemag.org/content/347/6223/1259855** (accessed 5 February 2021).
3   I. Angus, 'The photosynthetic ceiling: don't duck your head just yet', *Climate and Capitalism* blog (16 March 2008), **climateandcapitalism. com/2008/03/16/the-photosynthetic-ceiling-dont-duck-your-head-just-yet** (accessed 20 May 2020).
4   M. Lynas, *The God Species: How the planet can survive the age of humans* (Fourth Estate, 2011).
5   M.J. Hodson and M.R. Hodson, *Cherishing the Earth: How to care for God's creation* (Monarch, 2008), pp. 48–52.
6   D. Walker and G. Cresswell, *Whales and Dolphins of the European Atlantic* (2nd edn) (WildGuides, 2008).
7   C.K. Pham et al., 'Marine litter distribution and density in European seas, from the shelves to deep basins' *PLoS ONE* 9, no. 4 (2014), **journals.plos.org/plosone/article?id=10.1371/journal. pone.0095839** (accessed 20 May 2020).
8   R. Sider, *Rich Christians in an Age of Hunger* (IVP, 1977).
9   See, for example, R. Bauckham, *Bible and Ecology: Rediscovering the community of creation* (DLT, 2010) and Hodson and Hodson, *Cherishing the Earth*.
10 A Rocha, **arocha.org/en** (accessed 20 May 2020).
11 A Rocha UK, **arocha.org.uk** (accessed 20 May 2020).
12 The John Ray Initiative, **jri.org.uk** (accessed 20 May 2020).

2 BIODIVERSITY

The Hula Valley

One October we were in northern Israel. We do not consider ourselves bird experts, but we knew that this was a key time for migratory birds and we definitely wanted to see some. The Hula Valley, north of the Sea of Galilee, is a particularly good place for watching birds as they stop there to rest and stock up on their long journeys. The highlight of our visit was undoubtedly our safari trip out on to the marshes at the Agamon Hula reserve. The reserve has special tractor-drawn observation galleries, which are taken out on to the swamp. Apparently the birds are so used to tractors in nearby agricultural fields that they take no notice.

It was nearing dusk when we set out, and the birds were very active, getting ready to roost on the shallow waters. They were not the only active creatures and we also saw coypu, swamp cat and wild boar. The birds included spoonbill, pelican and ibis, but it was the cranes that were the most spectacular, and they also have an interesting story to tell. Eurasian cranes (*Grus grus*) are migratory birds that breed in the north and overwinter mostly in Africa.[1] Although cranes are not a threatened species, they have become extinct in parts of their range (including most of the United Kingdom) and have declined in other areas. The main threat to the species comes from habitat loss and degradation, including agricultural expansion and the drainage of wetlands, but they have also been affected by pesticides, egg collection and shooting.

In the 1950s Israel had a major push to increase its agricultural production, including draining much of the wetland in the Hula Valley. This also had the advantage of decreasing habitats for mosquitoes that carried malaria. But it was very bad news for the cranes and other migratory birds that used the valley as a stopping place en route back and forth between their breeding grounds and winter quarters. Draining the Hula Valley had some other unintended consequences. Chemical fertilisers used on the land began flowing into the Sea of Galilee, lowering its water quality. The soil that had lost its vegetation cover began to blow away through wind erosion. The drained swamps exposed peat soils, which often ignited spontaneously, and the resulting underground fires were difficult to put out.

Part of the valley was restored as swampland in the early 1990s, and the migratory birds soon returned, using the site as a stopover. The cranes found the nearby peanut crops much to their liking and some decided that they no longer needed to fly further south and overwintered in Israel. The crane population has also grown in recent years, so now there is a need to encourage the cranes on their way south. The Crane Project in the Hula Valley[2] is trying to do this, and it involves cooperation between several agencies, farmers and environmentalists. This whole story well illustrates just how complex environmental systems are, and that human changes to a system can give unexpected results.

Biodiversity facts

Biodiversity is one of our major concerns at the moment. Essentially it is a term that includes the variation in all of the plants, animals and other organisms on the planet. Biodiversity varies with the region and tropical areas are more diverse than temperate areas, which in turn are more diverse than Arctic areas. We are still not sure how many organisms share our planet with us. We have certainly discovered most of the large animal and plant species. Birds are a particularly well-known class of animals, and only five or six new species are being described a year. However, surprising discoveries are still being made. Early in 2020, Frank Rheindt and his colleagues found five new song-bird species and five new subspecies on a single small island near Sulawesi, Indonesia.[3] One creature that made the news in June 2013 (which we did not see on our visit to the Hula Valley) was the Hula painted frog.[4] This 'living fossil' had not been seen for 60 years, and it was assumed that it had been a victim of the drainage of the marshes. So it was not a totally new discovery, but still a surprising one.

Biodiversity loss

Biodiversity is amazing, and we are discovering more of it every year, but it is also under serious threat. Biodiversity loss is occurring at a rate far above the 'natural rate' seen in the geological record, maybe 1,000 times faster. Scientists often talk of this as the sixth great extinction event. The previous five events have all been observed in geological history and were caused by natural phenomena. The last extinction event was brought about by an asteroid hitting the Yucatan Peninsula in Mexico some 65 million years ago and was responsible for wiping out the dinosaurs. The present event has been entirely caused by humanity. The International Year of Biodiversity in 2010 coincided with the target year adopted by the Parties to the Convention on Biological Diversity at the World Summit for Sustainable Development in Johannesburg in 2002. When they looked at the targets set in 2002, governments had to admit that they had failed to limit biodiversity loss. In 2020 the WWF reported that population sizes of vertebrates have shown an average drop of 68% between 1970 and 2016.[5]

Reasons for biodiversity loss

How have humans impacted on biodiversity? Biologist Edward O. Wilson introduced the acronym HIPPO, which stands for habitat destruction, invasive species, pollution, human overpopulation and overharvesting. He considered that these were the major reasons for the decline in biodiversity, and we will now briefly consider each in turn.

Habitat destruction

There is little doubt that, so far, it is loss of habitat that has caused the greatest decline in biodiversity. As we saw above, the loss of their habitat was a major problem for the cranes in the Hula Valley, as the area was drained in the 1950s. After draining, 119 animal species were lost to the region, and 37 of those were completely lost from Israel.[6] Several aquatic plant species also disappeared at the time. It is often difficult to be certain that a species is extinct, however, as the case of the Hula painted frog well illustrates. After the partial restoration, the cranes flourished once more, and so did a number of other plant and animal species.

Ever since humans began to practise agriculture 10,000 years ago, they have been modifying natural habitats for this purpose. Now cultivated systems account for about a third of the land surface area of our planet, or about half of the total habitable land.[7] Agricultural land is also steadily being turned over to urban usage. Many urban environments are even less good for biodiversity than agriculture.

Invasive species

Invasive species are mostly non-native animals and plants that have been introduced from other parts of the world. When this happens, many species find the new environment problematic and do not get a foothold, but a few thrive and become invasive. The coypu that we saw in the Hula Valley were introduced accidentally from Argentina. The species was brought to Israel in the 20th century with the idea of setting up fur farms. This was not a success, however, as in Israel's hot climate the coypu did not produce good-quality fur. Moreover, a number of coypu escaped into the wild, bred, and established populations in suitable habitats such as the Hula Valley. The same happened in the United Kingdom, where coypu were causing quite big problems by burrowing into river banks and damaging crops. They became very common in East Anglia but never really took to British winters, during which many died or suffered frostbite. This meant that when a determined campaign to eliminate the coypu in the United Kingdom began, it had help from the winter weather, and the last coypu was shot in 1989.

In autumn 2014, on our sabbatical, we were in southern Spain and decided to visit the famous Doñana National Park. One day we walked around El Acebuche, a coastal lagoon which was very dry at the time as the rainy season had only just begun.[8] We saw some azure-winged magpies, but the wetland birds would arrive only in the next month or so as the lagoon filled. In common with many of the other wetland areas that we visited, there were signs up warning people not to release exotic animals and plants, and there were obviously particular worries about turtles. Ten years previously, a group of Spanish scientists had conducted a study of the ecology of the invasive red-eared slider (*Trachemys scripta elegans*) at El Acebuche.[9] The slider is a North American species that is a popular pet in many parts of the world but has been released into the wild in some countries and become a problem. In southern Spain it competes with two vulnerable native species of aquatic turtle (*Emys orbicularis* and *Mauremys leprosa*).

Pollution

One factor that was probably responsible for the decline in numbers of Eurasian cranes was poisoning with an organo-chlorine insecticide, DDT (dichlorodiphenyltrichloroethane). We say 'probably' as, despite an extensive web and literature database search, we have only been able to find anecdotal evidence involving this species. For other crane species worldwide, the picture seems clearer. The insecticidal properties of DDT were discovered in 1939 and it was used to control malaria-carrying mosquitoes during World War II. Later it was used in agriculture and would certainly have been used to control mosquitoes in the Hula Valley, which was notorious for malaria infections. Rachel Carson's *Silent Spring*,[10] which was published in 1962, suggested that DDT was toxic to birds and mammals, including humans. The DDT passed up the food chain and accumulated in fat, and the birds laid eggs with thin shells. The chemical had a particularly bad effect on birds of prey that were at the top of the food chain, but was also found in species as diverse as blue tits and penguins. Eventually a worldwide ban on the use of DDT in agriculture was brought in.

Humans have accidentally or deliberately introduced numerous other chemical substances into the environment, and many have bad effects on biodiversity. We have already mentioned that pollution from fertilisers was another problem that affected the Sea of Galilee as a result of draining the Hula Valley.

Human overpopulation

We will consider human population in more detail in chapter 5, but here we should note that the increase in population has indirectly caused a decline in biodiversity, as humans need land for agriculture and to live on. Again the Hula Valley provides a good example. The reason it was drained in the 1950s was largely to increase agricultural production and to provide food security for the growing Israeli population, many of whom had migrated to Israel during and after World War II.

Overharvesting

Overharvesting includes phenomena such as hunting, collection for the pet trade, and overexploitation of fish stocks. Almost certainly, hunting was a major factor in the decrease in crane populations in England, which eventually led to extinction there. In recent years there have been some attempts to reintroduce cranes into England, and now a small number of pairs are attempting to breed. Hunting is still a big problem for crane flocks that migrate through Afghanistan and Pakistan.[11]

One bird species that was affected far more by hunting than the crane was the passenger pigeon (*Ectopistes migratorius*).[12] This was a North American bird that suffered from both habitat destruction and hunting in the 19th century. It was a very common bird: its flocks were often numbered in their millions. This flocking behaviour was part of the downfall of the species, however, as it was easy to hunt. Highly mechanised hunting provided a cheap source of meat for the poor and for the large slave population at that time. Hunting led to the complete collapse of the passenger pigeon population. Desperate attempts were made to breed from the last few individuals, but it was discovered that the birds only bred successfully when in large flocks. The last known pigeon, Martha, died on 1 September 1914 in Cincinnati Zoo.

Climate change

When we visited the Hula Valley, climate change came up in our conversations concerning the relatively new phenomenon of cranes overwintering in Israel. We concluded that milder winters in Israel might influence crane migratory patterns, but that the peanuts provided by the local farmers might be a greater factor! When Wilson coined the HIPPO acronym, climate change was not seen as such an important factor in affecting biodiversity, but that is no longer the case. Climate change will be covered in more detail in chapter 3, but here we will focus on its effects on biodiversity, as it has already caused quite big changes.[13] In the United Kingdom we have seen earlier spring bud burst, flowering, insect emergence and egg laying. There is also good evidence that some animal species are changing their range in response to warming temperatures. At the moment there is no definite proof that any plant or animal has become extinct solely or largely owing to human-induced climate change. Scientists are, however, worried that the speed of climate change later in this century could indeed lead to mass extinctions, as plants and animals may be unable to adapt or shift range fast enough.

Covid-19 and biodiversity

Is there a connection between the Covid-19 pandemic and our dreadful treatment of the natural world? Many scientists believe that this is probably the case. There are three main hypotheses for the origins of the coronavirus SARS-CoV-2, the virus behind Covid-19: that it was genetically modified in a laboratory; that it was a natural virus being investigated in a laboratory; and that it jumped from bats to humans in the wild, possibly via an intermediary.

As we write, in summer 2020, most scientists do not consider genetic modification very likely. The laboratory-escape hypothesis is considered a low probability compared with a zoonosis (where the virus moves from one host to humans). A number of previous pandemics have arisen through zoonosis, either from domesticated animals or from 'spill over' events in the wild. For many years there have been worries concerning the wild-animal trade, and that the markets selling these animals might be places where these events might occur. The, often rare, animals are frequently kept in cramped insanitary conditions. SARS-CoV-2 is most closely related to viruses found in bats, and it is thought that the virus somehow made the jump to infect humans. It is not at all certain how this might have occurred, but it seems likely that it was in another animal. The SARS outbreak in 2003 was eventually found to have been caused by SARS-CoV-1, which came from bats via civet cats. Governments have been rapidly trying to close down wild-animal markets since the Covid-19 outbreak.

Whatever the sources of SARS-CoV-2, it is very clear that it is not a random act of God (a 'natural evil'), and that human agency was behind it.[14]

Rewilding

There is a growing number of projects that seek to reintroduce species to areas where they used to thrive but were lost through human activity, such as hunting and clearing woodland for agriculture. Some introductions have been very successful: 2020 marked 30 years since the reintroduction of red kites to Buckinghamshire and they are now a common sight across a wide region. There was also exciting news in April 2020 of white stork eggs hatching in the wild in Britain for the first time in 600 years! These had been part of a reintroduction programme on the Knepp Estate in West Sussex and a breeding programme at the Cotswold Wildlife Park (part of our own benefice in Oxfordshire), together with other partners.[15]

More controversial has been the reintroduction of larger mammals. Wolves and bears have been reintroduced to a number of regions in Europe, including the Pyrenees. These have divided opinion with huge support from wildlife conservationists but consternation among the sheep-farming community. After several years of sheep losses, this culminated in the shooting of a (protected) bear in June 2020.[16]

Rewilding can help to restore balance in ecosystems: in August 2020, conservationists were delighted to hear that beavers in Devon were given 'leave to remain' by the government. These 'appeared' in the River Otter in 2013 and Devon Wildlife Trust secured a five-year trial to measure their impacts on the local environment. Their 2020 report concluded that the beavers dam-building helped reduce flooding risk for some homes and created wetlands that provided habitats for other species, including endangered water voles. They also improved water quality. There were downsides in terms of damage to trees and flooding of parts of fields, but the Wildlife Trust found these could be managed with suitable support for farmers. In 2020 there were 15 family groups of beavers along the River Otter, and it has been ruled that these can stay and extend their range naturally.[17] Conservationists would now like to see beaver introductions to other parts of the country, along with other species. A planned reintroduction of bison to Kent in 2022 is hoped to achieve positive impacts on local habitats.[18]

Biblical reflection: How much is nature worth?

Former *Guardian* journalist Leo Hickman has asked the question, 'Can we afford to save species from extinction?'[19] He suggests that it is going to cost £50 billion a year, worldwide, to protect the world's endangered species from extinction. If we value nature purely in monetary terms, we find a pragmatic set of reasons to preserve nature. One reason, Hickman argues, is to maintain the robustness of our global ecosystems. If we knock out too many links in our global ecology, we may find that our own life support machine will collapse. Hickman concludes, 'Can we afford not to? These habitats also support… the one species that has the power, means and comprehension to decide their fate. Why do I have that image in my head of the man in the silent movie sawing away at the branch in the tree upon which he sits?'

Another reason to conserve nature is to preserve as broad a genetic pool as possible to provide for pharmaceuticals and agricultural research. Each time a species becomes extinct, its genetic material is lost to the future world. Other people want to preserve nature for tourism and for the use of the species, either for food or for other resources that may be of value. A further reason would be the protection that nature gives to humans. Environmentalist Tony Juniper has used an economic approach to argue that many natural features are far more valuable than the economic initiatives that replace them.[20] One example is mangroves, which grow in shallow waters and have been cleared in many places for shrimp farming to boost local economies. The problem is that the mangroves gave storm protection to the villages and towns on the coastlines. Juniper calculates that constructing artificial sea defences could cost 100 times more than the revenue from the shrimp farms.

So there are plenty of practical reasons to protect nature and save plants and animals from extinction, but they are all for the sake of humans. If economics are the only measure of value, then we will also have a hierarchy of value in the biological world. Plants and animals that are of special value to tourism will score high, as will (human) food species and plants of known medicinal value. At the top will be large and beautiful mammals, attractive birds and commercial fish. Near the bottom will be unattractive insects and reptiles.

This may all seem a crude and utilitarian way to view nature but, inevitably, economics often dominate the way humans interact with the natural world. In 2005 the Millennium Ecosystem Assessment popularised the term 'ecosystem services' to explain the value of ecosystems to humans and to encourage conservation of ecosystems for the benefit of human populations. TEEB (The Economics of Ecosystems and Biodiversity) was developed a few years later to promote the economic value of biodiversity that is lost when nature is destroyed.

These initiatives use economic arguments because they know that these are likely to be taken more seriously by leaders of the world's nations and economies. However, conservationists have a far deeper understanding of the value of nature than simply placing it within a balance sheet. What are the other ways of valuing nature? Philosophers start by asking the question 'Valuable to whom?' If we stick with 'valuable to humans', but put aside economics, we might start to look at ideals of beauty and human well-being. Michael Winter takes this approach and suggests that human well-being is greatly improved with access to healthy natural environments.[21] This feels more ethical than monetary approaches but it is still anthropocentric. Does nature have a value only in relation to humans? To move beyond the value to humanity, we need to consider whether nature can have an intrinsic value. Does there always need to be someone to value it? For people of faith, we start by asking the question, 'Has nature any value to God?'

Job encounters the creator God

One book of the Bible that especially considers God's view of nature is Job. From chapter 38 onwards, the Lord uses nature in a dialogue with the suffering Job, to put his questions into context. The writer of the book does not paint a picture of a cosmos that has been created for the benefit of humans. On the contrary, these majestic chapters portray a God who delights in his creation, which is beyond the comprehension of humanity: 'Can you bind the chains of the Pleiades? Can you loosen Orion's belt?… Do you know when the mountain goats give birth? Do you watch when the doe bears her fawn? Do you count the months till they bear?' (Job 38:31; 39:1–2).[22]

When we teach environmental ethics, we encourage students to move beyond anthropocentric ethics, where we see everything in the light of its usefulness to ourselves. We explain the value of ecocentric ethics, where the benefit to the overall ecosystem is central to decision making, and biocentric ethics, where each individual organism is seen to be of value.[23] In Job we see a biocentric God who has created a perfectly balanced universe for the sheer joy of it. In this we find the answer to the question, 'Valuable to whom?' Nature has value because it is valuable to the God who created it. This theocentric ethic provides our base point for decisions about global biodiversity.

Nature and the place of humans

An ethical view known as Deep Ecology is one of the most biocentric of all the approaches to nature. It holds the value of each individual organism as paramount and is deeply critical of humanity's abuse of the natural world. This deep green ethic was first proposed by Norwegian philosopher Arne Naess in 1973. Naess believed that humanity needed to hold back from their use of nature, to enable other species to flourish. He advocated simple living and population control for humans and considered that all species had an equal right to space on the planet. The strength of deep ecology is that it does not see a hierarchy in creation: a small, ugly insect is seen as of equal value to a large, beautiful bird or mammal. It proposes the interconnectedness of all things. People are encouraged to grasp this as a starting point to greater self-understanding and changed behaviour.

This view of nature and humanity has been criticised for being utopian and also for treating humans as just another species with the same rights as any other. Ironically, the call for humans to modify their behaviour exposes a view of humanity as distinct from other species. We are the only creatures on Earth who have the foresight and ability to be able to analyse the future and change our behaviour accordingly.

To explore these concepts from a Christian perspective, we must touch briefly on the most classic biblical creation text, Genesis 1. In this chapter the intrinsic value of nature is set out. After each day of creating, God looks at what he has created and declares that it is good. The God who set out his love of nature to Job is portrayed here in the act of lovingly creating it. In the Bible, the number seven has a special significance: it is used to show something that is perfect. In Genesis 1, the word 'good' is used seven times. The chapter ends with the creation of humans and the seventh 'good', which has an additional adverb making it 'very good'. So this passage teaches that humans are part of God's creation. God sees creation as good, but, with the creation of humans, the seventh 'good' is reached and God sees it as 'very good'. Why is this? The writer explains that God created human-ity in his image and gave us responsibility for the rest of creation. Our wonderful and fearful role as part of God's creation is to have leader-ship. Have we been faithful so far?

A Rocha Lebanon

In the mid-1990s A Rocha began an initiative to preserve the Aammiq wetland in Lebanon's Bekaa Valley.[24] North of the Hula wetland in Israel, the Aammiq wetland is another vital stopping-point for birds migrating on the migratory superhighway between Europe and Africa.

Not needing passports, the birds are oblivious to the political tensions between the two nations. The Aammiq wetland is Lebanon's most important remaining natural freshwater site, a rarity in the Middle East. The wetland was under threat but, thanks to the work of A Rocha Lebanon, the damage has been reversed and it is now protected. A Rocha worked with the landowning family and local agricultural-ists to promote crops needing less water. This reduced the need for irrigation and helped to prevent the marshes drying out. An important element in getting public support has been the creation of a highly popular organic restaurant overlooking the wetland. The Aammiq wetland, now a designated Ramsar site,[25] is 20 per cent bigger than it was in 1997. In addition to the conservation work, A Rocha Lebanon developed a major educational programme for school and university students. Some 6,000 students have been through this programme and this should lead to a greater appreciation of nature, securing protection for Aammiq into the future.[26]

Human responsibility to care for the Earth

In this chapter we have exposed a crisis with the rest of biodiversity, and we need to ask the question 'Why?' We believe it is because we have not totally understood what it means to be both fully part of this world and also made in God's image. If we behave as if we are simply part of creation and not different from other species, we can forget our responsibility to the rest of creation. We put our species first and tend to be short-term in our thinking. Following this route will eventually lead humanity to consume itself into extinction as the world's resources are used up and global ecosystems collapse under the strain (chapter 5). This is the route that many believe our material-ist modern economies are taking.

At the opposite end of the spectrum, we carry a legacy of a 'spiritual-ised' form of Christian faith in the west, which saw humans as made in God's image and destined for a higher spiritual world. This teaching plays down the role of humans as part of creation, seeing this world as something negative, to be escaped from. This very spiritual interpretation of the Christian faith inevitably leads to an understanding of dominion that takes a dismissive view of the natural world. With this viewpoint, people have felt able to pollute and damage the world, believing that God is interested only in a higher spiritual realm. If we can grasp the truth that humanity is part of creation and made in God's image, there is hope that we will see far enough ahead to change our behaviour and work towards environmental sustainability. We need to take our leadership of creation seriously.

 It is very rewarding to create a habitat. If you have a garden, you might like to start to nurture native plants that will encourage biodiversity. Other ideas might be to install a bird nesting box, a hedgehog box or a 'bug hotel'. If you are in an apartment or a student room, why not see if your church, or even your college, might install some swift boxes.

Bible study: creation in God's commandments

When we think of the ten commandments, we usually think of them as a set of 'dos' and 'don'ts' for 'us humans' to obey in relating to each other and to God. However, the ten commandments also say things about how God values his creation and how he wants us to relate to it. These words are not spoken to the whole of humanity but to God's chosen people, whom he has rescued from slavery. They are a set of covenant guidelines and they clarify God's ideal for relationships between himself, his people and the rest of his creation. The first three commandments focus on our relationship with God, the fourth commandment affects all three sets of relationships, and the final six primarily have an impact on our relationships with one another.

Read Exodus 20:1–7

1 What can we learn about God's relationship with his created world?
2 What relationship does God want to have with his people, and how is this relationship maintained?

Read Exodus 20:8–11

3 What does the commandment to 'keep the sabbath' say about our relationship with the living world?
4 What does the sabbath commandment say about God's value for creation?

Read Exodus 20:12–17

5 These six commandments are about respect in relationships and speak primarily about human relationships with one another. In what ways is our relationship with God and the material world important in these commandments?

Understanding God's relationship with creation and our role in protecting and sustaining his world leads us to see some familiar Bible passages with fresh eyes. Their teaching about relationships between God, humans and one another is no less important, but an environmental dimension is there if we look for it. You may like to end by thinking of one or two other Bible passages where relationships with creation are implicit in the meaning of the text.

Notes

1 H. Shirihai, *The Birds of Israel* (Academic Press, 1996), pp. 164–65.

2 Agamon Hula, 'The crane project in the Hula Valley', **agamon-hula. co.il/?lang=en_US** (accessed 4 July 2020).

3 F.E. Rheindt et al., 'A lost world in Wallacea: description of a montane archipelagic avifauna', *Science* 367 (2020), pp. 167–170. **science. sciencemag.org/content/367/6474/167** (accessed 5 February 2021).

4 R. Morelle, 'Rediscovered Hula painted frog "is a living fossil"', *BBC News* (4 June 2013), **bbc.co.uk/news/science-environment-22770959** (accessed 4 July 2020).

5 WWF, *Living Planet Report 2020: Bending the curve of biodiversity loss*, R.E.A. Almond, M. Grooten and T. Petersen (eds) (WWF, 2020).

6 Jewish Virtual Library, *Geography of Israel: Hula Valley*, **jewishvirtuallibrary.org/hula-valley** (accessed 4 July 2020).

7 H. Ritchie and M. Roser, 'Land use', **ourworldindata.org/land-use** (accessed 4 July 2020).

8 Donana Parque Nacional, '1. The Acebuche paths', **discoveringdonana.com/descargas/ingles/acebuche.pdf** (accessed 4 July 2020).

9 N. Perez-Santigosa, C. Diaz-Paniagua and J. Hidalgo-Vila, 'The reproductive ecology of exotic *Trachemys scripta elegans* in an invaded area of southern Europe', *Aquatic Conservation: Marine and Freshwater Ecosystems* 18 (2008), pp. 1302–10.

10 R. Carson, *Silent Spring* (Houghton Mifflin, 1962).

11 'Common crane *Grus grus*', Birdlife International, **datazone.birdlife. org/species/factsheet/22692146** (accessed 4 July 2020).

12 'Passenger pigeon', Wikipedia, **en.wikipedia.org/wiki/Passenger_ Pigeon** (accessed 4 July 2020).

13 M.D. Morecroft and L. Speakman (eds), *Biodiversity Climate Change Impacts Summary Report* (Living with Environmental Change, 2015), **nerc.ukri.org/research/partnerships/ride/lwec/report-cards/ biodiversity** (accessed 4 July 2020).

14 For more on this topic see: R. Valerio, M.J. Hodson, M.R. Hodson and T. Howles, *Covid-19: Environment, justice, and the future* (Grove, Cambridge, 2020)

15 Further information about the white stork project can be found at **whitestorkproject.org** (accessed 27 July 2020).

16 'Pyrenees bear found shot dead in southwest France', *The Connexion*, 10 June 2020, **connexionfrance.com/French-news/Pyrenees-bear-**

found-shot-dead-in-southwest-France-prompting-condemnation-from-State-and-campaigners (accessed 31 August 2020)

17 E. Beament, 'Beavers given leave to remain', *Ecologist: The journal for the post-industrial age*, 6 August 2020, **theecologist.org/2020/aug/06/beavers-given-leave-remain** (accessed 31 August 2020)

18 S. Moss, 'Missing lynx: how rewilding Britain could restore its natural balance', *The Observer*, 12 July 2020, **theguardian.com/environment/2020/jul/12/missing-lynx-how-rewilding-britain-could-restore-its-natural-balance** (accessed 27 July 2020).

19 L. Hickman, 'Can we afford to save species from extinction?' *The Guardian*, 12 October 2012, **theguardian.com/environment/blog/2012/oct/12/extinction-species-save-cost-biodiversity** (accessed 28 July 2020).

20 A. Juniper, *What Has Nature Ever Done for Us? How money really does grow on trees* (Profile Books, 2013).

21 M. Winter, 'The land and human well-being', in A. Smith and J. Hopkinson (eds), *Faith and the Future of the Countryside* (Canterbury Press, 2012), pp. 24–44.

22 J.J. Bimson, *The Book of Job and Environmental Ethics: The message from the whirlwind* (Grove, Cambridge, 2020).

23 M.J. Hodson and M.R. Hodson, *An Introduction to Environmental Ethics* (Grove, Cambridge, 2017).

24 See P. Harris, *Kingfisher's Fire: A story of hope for God's Earth* (Monarch, 2008), pp. 81–92; A Rocha Lebanon, **arocha.org/en/a-rocha-lebanon** (accessed 14 May 2020).

25 Ramsar sites are wetlands of international importance, designated under the Ramsar Convention. See **ramsar.org** (accessed 14 May 2020).

26 For a personal insight into the founding of A Rocha Lebanon, see Chris Naylor, *Postcards from the Middle East* (Lion, 2015). Sadly, Chris Naylor died in 2019, and we are grateful to Dr Chris Walley, the co-founder of A Rocha Lebanon, for updating this section.

3 CLIMATE CHANGE

Hope for Planet Earth

On 3 May 2007, I (Martin) finished a lecture at Oxford Brookes University and then sprinted for the coach to London. Once in the city, I grabbed a taxi to Westminster Hall, the Methodist headquarters. I was attending my first planning meeting for a national climate change tour that was scheduled for spring 2008, and I was representing The John Ray Initiative (JRI). The meeting was chaired by Methodist evangelist Rob Frost, the head of Share Jesus International (SJI), and there were also representatives from A Rocha UK and Tearfund. The tour was the brainchild of Rob Frost and Sir John Houghton. Over the following months, we had numerous planning meetings and discussions. It was agreed that each of the four organisations would concentrate on a 15-minute slot, and JRI was allocated the first one, on the science of climate change. So over the winter months I collaborated with Sir John, putting together our section. Sadly, while we were preparing for the tour, Rob Frost became ill and eventually died of cancer, a very sad loss. But we continued with the preparations, sure that Rob would have wanted us to do so. Rob's son, Andy Frost, took up the reins of SJI and also took Rob's place on the tour.

After months of planning and publicity, on 18 February 2008 the 'Hope for Planet Earth' tour began in Stoke. We spent four weeks on the road and visited 20 venues. The tour took us to schools during the day and (largely) Christian audiences in the evenings, after which we would pack up and drive through the night to our next venue. The wonderful

team from SJI sorted the logistics so that we were not zigzagging all over the country. The tour went really well and we did another one in 2009, this time getting up to Scotland. In the course of the tours we spoke to thousands of children and adults. As with many such events, we will never know the full impact, but we hope that we helped inform people about the realities of climate change.[1] One of the unexpected bonuses was that the staff from JRI, SJI, A Rocha UK and Tearfund developed really strong relationships, which persist to this day. Little did we know how much time we would spend in action on climate change over the next ten years.

The science of climate change

Climate change is the most serious threat to humanity this century. It is important to note that it is not the only threat, and several others covered in this book could cause us real trouble in the future. Quite simply, though, if we get climate change wrong, it will magnify all the other problems and things could spin out of control.

The greenhouse effect has been known about for over 100 years. Certain gases (carbon dioxide, methane, nitrous oxide, water vapour and a few minor components) act as a blanket within the atmosphere. The sun's radiation warms the Earth, but some of the heat is trapped by these gases, which keeps the Earth's surface much warmer than it would otherwise be. Since the Industrial Revolution, we have been burning increasing amounts of fossil fuels (and burning more and more trees during deforestation) and this has increased the concentration of carbon dioxide in the atmosphere. Carbon dioxide concentration has increased from 280 ppm before the Industrial Revolution to 416 ppm in 2020. This might be expected to cause an increase in temperature, and an approximately 1.0°C rise has been observed.

If we wish to consider the present state of the science of climate change, the Intergovernmental Panel on Climate Change (IPCC) is a good place to start.[2] Their fifth report was released in 2013 and 2014.

The physical science component of the report suggested that it is extremely likely (more than 95 per cent probability) that most of the observed increase in global average surface temperature from 1951 to 2010 was caused by humans. Scientists are also confident that this has led to warming of the oceans, melting of snow and ice, a rise in global mean sea level and the experience of more climate extremes with increased intensity. We will now look at each of these phenomena in turn, concentrating our attention on some of the most recent findings.

Climate change and its impacts

It is now certain that global surface temperature rose in the last century by about 1.0°C. Most scientists attribute this rise almost entirely to our increased greenhouse gas emissions. Nearly all of the hottest years in the instrumental record have been since the turn of the millennium. It is not well known, but over 90 per cent of the heat from global warming has been warming the oceans, not the Earth's surface, and ocean temperatures have also been rising steadily. This is a serious problem because warmer oceans impart more energy to weather systems, such as hurricanes.

Meanwhile, the melting of glaciers and ice caps has continued apace. An excellent visual demonstration of just how fast glaciers are melting was produced by cameraman James Balog, and his story is told in the film *Chasing Ice*.[3] In the film, Balog and his team set up cameras to take regular photos of glaciers in the Arctic over several years. The results were visually stunning but extremely worrying, as most of the glaciers were retreating very rapidly. Even since we wrote the first edition of this book in 2014, the Arctic ice cap has decreased further in size. The summer of 2019 was particularly worrying, and the ice cap decreased to its second-lowest size since 1979, when satellite monitoring started.[4] On 18 July 2020, it was 26 per cent lower than the historical average for the day. A tanker, the *Christophe de Margerie*, set sail from Sabetta, a northern Russian port, on 18 May 2020, and took less than three weeks to reach the Chinese port of Yangkou. This was the earliest date a cargo ship had ever taken the route that is usually blocked by ice. Ice may well disappear in the summer within the next few decades.

Sea level rise has, so far, had relatively minor effects, but the impacts are expected to increase this century. Two processes are responsible: the expansion of sea water as global temperature increases and the melting of land-based ice caps and glaciers. Recent work by Nerem and colleagues[5] has suggested that global mean sea level rose by about 3 mm per year since 1993, and the rate is accelerating by 0.084 mm per year. This would suggest that globally sea level will rise by about 65 cm by 2100 if we do not see major changes such as a rapid collapse of the Antarctic ice shelf. The authors therefore suggest that their estimate of a 65 cm rise should be seen as a conservative minimum, and that greater rises are certainly possible.

Anecdotal evidence suggests that the number and severity of extreme weather events around the world is increasing, but are any of these events caused by human-induced climate change? The relatively new field of 'extreme event attribution' is now beginning to provide the answers to these questions. The scientists at CarbonBrief summarised progress in this field in 2020, looking at more than 355 peer-reviewed papers.[6] Of the extreme weather events considered, 69 per cent were found to be made more likely or severe by climate change, 9 per cent were made less likely or less severe, and in 22 per cent there was no obvious human influence. Extreme heat was investigated in 125 studies, and 93 per cent found that climate change made the event more likely. Rainfall or flooding was looked at in 68 studies, and 54 per cent found human activity had made the event more likely or more severe. Of the 61 drought events, 61 per cent were more likely or severe because of climate change. It does seem likely that the intensity of hurricanes is increasing,[7] but maybe not their number. Tornadoes are also probably increasing in power, but it is not yet certain that this is due to climate change.[8]

Hot, dry weather often leads to an increase in wildfires. This certainly happened in Australia in 2019–20, when terrible fires decimated large areas of the country and killed many animals and plants. It is estimated that climate change boosted the risk of these fires by at least 30 per cent.[9]

When disasters happen, it is nearly always the poor who suffer disproportionately from them, and this is certainly the case with climate-related events. Typhoon Haiyan,[10] which hit the Philippines on 8 November 2013, was devastating, causing at least 6,300 deaths, and many people lost their homes. The typhoon was one of the strongest storms ever to make landfall. It was strengthened as it tracked over an area of the Pacific that had very warm water.[11]

Ten years of ups and downs

It turned out that 2009, the year of the second 'Hope for Planet Earth' tour, was a significant year for us, as Margot began a new job as vicar of Haddenham benefice in Buckinghamshire.[12] We soon found ourselves involved in the local Transition group,[13] and Martin answered questions after several showings of *The Age of Stupid*, the climate change documentary drama film.[14] Late in 2009, activity on climate change ramped up in all sorts of ways. In 'Climategate', the server was hacked at the Climate Research Unit at the University of East Anglia and extracts of emails from scientists were released on to the internet, purporting to show that they had massaged their data to get the results they wanted. After several extensive investigations, the scientists were exonerated, but the damage had been done in the minds of the general public.[15]

In December 2009 we went on 'The Wave' climate change march in London with several thousand others, including many Christians. Then there was the huge disappointment that was the Copenhagen United Nations (UN) climate change COP15 meeting. Such high hopes had been raised that we would get a fair and binding agreement to limit carbon emissions, but in the end there was no deal. Quite why the world's leaders failed to agree a deal is a complex issue, but all those who had campaigned so hard for it were devastated. It is fair to say that before Copenhagen many environmentalists were hopeful that we could 'solve' the climate change problem, and that afterwards this hope tended to evaporate. The UN climate change process continued with the aim of reaching a global deal at the meeting in Paris in December 2015. COP21 in Paris had a considerably more positive outcome than the Copenhagen meeting.[16] The countries of the world were all invited to submit their plans for cutting carbon emissions. When almost all the countries had done so, the totals were added up, and it was clear that governments were not being ambitious enough. Copenhagen had set a target of 2.0°C above the pre-industrial temperature, but the plans submitted would lead to something around 3.0°C, well into dangerous territory. Moreover, some of the poorer countries and lower-lying island states at COP21 pushed for a new target of 1.5°C, and they gained agreement on this. The target would now be 'well below 2.0°C'. To tackle the ambition problem, governments would take part in a ratcheting mechanism, whereby they would come back every five years with revised, hopefully greater, emissions cuts. There was also some movement on funding for poorer nations, and on transparency in monitoring emissions cuts. But there was a lot else happening in Paris, with businesses, mayors, NGOs and faith groups all involved in their own meetings. Paris was hugely positive and kick-started a lot of changes in the energy sector (see chapter 6).

But there was a massive cloud on the horizon after Paris. I (Martin) learned of the election of Donald Trump as president of the United States while in Sweden in November 2016. I was with a delegation from Oxford Diocese who were visiting Växjö Diocese to see some of their environmental work and meet some of those behind it. It is fair to say that both our delegation and our Swedish friends were shocked by the election result. We all had a pretty good idea of what was likely to come. I came back from Sweden determined to monitor the impacts of Trump on the environment, and I wrote two briefing papers on this topic.[17] On 1 June 2017, Trump announced that the United States was withdrawing from the Paris Agreement. He was actually beginning the withdrawal process, but that could only be completed after the US election in November 2020. Needless to say, Trump's impact on climate change and the environment in general has been almost entirely negative. However, he was unable to stop the closure of coal-fired power stations, and this has meant that the US is almost on track with its Paris Agreement commitments (see chapter 6).

In 2019 the time came for us the leave Haddenham after over ten happy years. Our environmental work was growing rapidly, and we needed to find more time to devote to it. Margot applied for a half-time post as associate vicar in the Shill Valley and Broadshire bene-fice in West Oxfordshire; she was successful, and we moved to the village of Filkins in August. We were very sad to leave all our friends in Haddenham and Wychert Vale Benefice. We had started with four churches, and after ten years we had developed a larger benefice and a big team. Curates had trained with us and fresh expressions had started and grown. We had shared both joy and sadness with these communities and our lives would never be quite the same again. All kinds of environmental initiatives had flourished and on our very last service in St Mary's Haddenham, it was a great privilege to be able to celebrate achieving an Eco Church Bronze Award (see chapter 10 for more on Eco Church).

It was only seven months after we came to Filkins, in March 2020, that the Covid-19 pandemic arrived in the UK. Our rather frenetic speaking engagements rapidly came to a halt (at least until everyone discovered Zoom) but organising and writing sped up. We spent some time monitoring the environmental implications of the pandemic, and out of this came a Grove booklet called *Covid-19: Environment, justice, and the future*.[18] Countries around the world went into lockdown, and at their peak CO_2 emissions dropped by a maximum of 26 per cent.[19] It is probable that this will cause the largest-ever annual cut in emissions (4 to 7 per cent relative to 2019). Most likely 2019 will prove to be the year with the historical global peak in annual emissions, and they will never again reach the same heights. The question now is how quickly we can bring emissions down, and will it be quickly enough to avert catastrophe.

While I (Martin) was still in Haddenham in 2018, I was invited by Professor Denis Alexander of the Faraday Institute to update a climate change briefing paper that had been written by Sir John Houghton some ten years earlier. The intention was to include this in a book containing many of the briefings from the Institute. By that time Sir John was suffering from memory difficulties, and it was clear that he would not be able to update it himself. I checked with him that he agreed with me doing the update, and he did, provided that he read it before publication! Fortunately, Sir John liked my work, and it went to press, coming out in November 2019.[20] I knew that it would almost certainly be his last publication, and it was a great honour to have been involved in it. Sir John Houghton died of complications from Covid-19 on 15 April 2020. I wrote his JRI obituary, which was published the following day.[21] Beneath it I appended all the other tributes and obituaries I could find. The IPCC have decided that the Working Group I contribution to the Sixth Assessment Report, *Climate Change 2021: The physical science basis*, will be dedicated to the memory of Sir John. He was a world-leading climate scientist, a visionary, a very committed Christian and a humble man. Sir John was simply the greatest man we have ever met.

US election 2020

Throughout 2020, the US election campaign was a dominant theme in our news. Former Vice President Joe Biden took on Donald Trump. The campaign was a bitter one, set against the backdrop of the Covid-19 pandemic, which was having a particularly bad effect in the United States. Climate change featured in the campaign as a topic for the first time, with Biden positive about taking action and Trump not at all. Biden had a whole raft of environmental policies that he intended to implement if elected.

On 3 November, the election finally happened. Biden won convincingly, in both electoral votes (306 to 232) and the popular vote. But Trump did not concede defeat and launched a series of unsuccessful law cases, based on flimsy evidence, trying to overturn the result in states where it was close. He convinced a large section of his supporters that the election was stolen from him. Things came to a head on 6 January 2021, when Congress were meeting in the Capitol Building in Washington DC to confirm the election result. Trump spoke at a rally in the city, and his supporters then attacked the Capitol Building, where five people died.

Joe Biden was inaugurated as the 46th president of the United States on 20 January 2021. He rapidly enacted executive orders to rejoin the Paris Agreement and to stop the Keystone XL pipeline. He appointed what Al Gore called an 'A+ team' to take forward his environmental agenda. Among them are John Kerry, special presidential envoy on climate change, and Gina McCarthy, head of the new White House Office of Climate Policy. Climate change was one of the top priorities of Biden's new administration, and this added to a generally positive international atmosphere as we approached the important COP26 meeting in Glasgow.[22]

The future

When we move on to consider climate change in the future we enter a zone of uncertainty. It is certain that, whatever we do now, the climate will continue to change and we will get more extreme weather events as a result. But it is highly unclear how bad things will get. A big part of the problem is that we do not know when or if humanity will take decisive action to deal with carbon emissions. So scientists have to account for many different scenarios when designing models to investigate future climate change. The most authoritative source for future predictions is the IPCC. Those who are sceptical of human-induced climate change say the IPCC is alarmist, while many environmentalists reckon it is too conservative in its predictions for the future.

In its 2013 report, the IPCC predicted a rise of at least 1.5°C relative to pre-industrial temperatures by the end of this century. That would imply approximately 0.5°C more than the temperature rise that has already occurred (1.0°C). At the time of the report, some latched on to the 1.5°C rise and implied that it was not as bad as it might be, but it should be stressed that this figure is a *minimum*. The rise could be much greater than that, particularly if we pass one or more of the 'tipping points'.[23] Most of the IPCC projections are based on straight lines and smooth curves, but we know from studies of past climates that abrupt changes do happen once a tipping point is reached. The snag with abrupt climate changes is that they are difficult to predict or model. What we do know is that the passing of tipping points becomes more likely, the greater the temperature rise.

One potential tipping point is the melting of the Arctic ice cap. As ice is white, it reflects incoming solar radiation, but the open water created by the melting of the ice cap absorbs the radiation and contributes to further warming of the oceans. Another tipping point concerns the permafrost in the sub-Arctic zones (such as Siberia). As the name suggests, this is permanently frozen ground, which thaws only slightly each summer as the warmer weather briefly melts the ice in the upper layers. When melting happens, bacteria begin to break down the organic matter in the soil, releasing methane. More warming leads to more methane being released. As methane is a powerful greenhouse gas, there is the potential that we could initiate a loop in which more warming leads to more methane production, which leads to more warming, and so on. We do not know the temperature at which these tipping points will click in, but it is fairly certain that anything much more than a 1.5°C rise above pre-industrial temperatures will be highly dangerous.

Many people were sceptical about whether the 1.5°C target, suggested at the COP21 meeting in Paris, was possible, and the UN commissioned the IPCC to write a special report on what would be needed to make this happen. The detailed report came out in 2018.[24] Essentially, it suggested that a 1.5°C target was possible, but only with drastic cuts in carbon emissions before 2030, and a whole range of other measures, particularly concerning carbon sequestration. The report also suggested that a rise of 1.5°C would be far preferable to one of 2.0°C, the original Copenhagen target. The IPCC is in the process of preparing its sixth assessment report, which is due out in 2021 or 2022, but there will almost certainly be some delays due to the Covid-19 pandemic. The report will probably not differ greatly from the fifth report in 2013, but there will be a greater level of certainty in many of the predictions. The UN climate change meeting, COP26, was due to be held in Glasgow in November 2020, but this was also delayed by the pandemic. It is now due to take pace in November 2021. That will be a crucial meeting, as governments will once again be asked to submit their plans for cutting emissions. Hopefully this ratcheting process will reveal that we are closer to the sort of cuts needed to avoid dangerous climate change.

We have already mentioned that it will be the world's poor people who suffer most from the effects of climate change, but what will happen to them? The late Norman Myers famously predicted that there could be over 200 million environmental refugees (people who have to move because of climate change) by 2050.[25] However, more recent research has suggested that migration due to climate change may not be so great, that most migration tends to be over short distances, and that the immobility of potential migrants may be as big a problem as their mobility.[26] Certainly, in the aftermath of Hurricane Katrina in 2005, it was the urban poor of New Orleans who were stranded in the city, while those with the means to do so had left for safety. The interaction between climate change, conflict and migration is understandably complex. Climate shocks, such as severe droughts and floods, initially tend to lead to movement within a country. Where this movement is combined with social discontent and conflict it can lead to migration over longer distances. Syria had severe drought in the years leading up to the civil war, and this led to migration from rural to urban areas. The civil war in 2011 led to a refugee crisis from Syria and also others impacted by the Arab Spring, particularly in northern Africa. How much climate change contributed to that continues to be debated.

Given all these complex factors, the level of migration we might see in the event of a total collapse of our civilisation remains an open question.[27]

There have been a number of fictional accounts of what might happen in the event of runaway climate change. In 2014, historians Naomi Oreskes and Erik Conway turned to fiction in *The Collapse of Western Civilization*.[28] In their short novel, a Chinese historian looks back at our century from 2393 and documents the events leading up to 'The Great Collapse' between 2073 and 2093. In the book, this refers first to a tipping point, the collapse of the Western Antarctic and Greenland ice sheets, which leads to a very rapid eight-metre sea level rise. It later comes to mean the complete collapse of our civilisation, accompanied by a mass migration of 1.5 billion people. Human population rapidly decreases, and only the release of a genetically engineered lichen, which quickly consumes carbon dioxide, rescues the remnants of humanity. This last event is probably the most unrealistic in the whole book. Oreskes and Conway have given us a prophecy concerning our possible future. Like the people of biblical times, it will be up to us to decide whether we heed the prophecy.

Biblical reflection: God's covenant with people and creation

The four churches in the village of Haddenham have a covenant with each other. Church members take it very seriously and it is something that the other village residents notice as they see the local Christians working together. Nationally, the Methodist Church has a special covenant service each year. This gives Christians the opportunity to renew their commitment to follow God in Christian service, whatever that might be and wherever it might lead. Covenant is a biblical concept, and we can find a progression of covenants in the Bible that concern our relationship with God, one another and creation. Today we tend to think of covenants as an agreement between equals, but in biblical times a covenant was more often initiated by a powerful person or nation who offered protection to a junior partner.[29] The relationship forged was intended to lead to mutual flourishing and be peace-giving in every possible way.

Covenant with creation

The word 'covenant' is not used in the account of creation but it is clear that God makes a commitment to his creation as he forms it. God created a world where all living things could flourish, and he gave humans leadership over creation and the ability to respond wisely. Some Christians have, at times in history, seen this covenant as being between God and humans alone. Creation, for them, is there merely to facilitate that relationship.[30] In chapter 1 we saw that creation reveals the glory of God and that all creation worships God. God made a commitment to the natural world through the very act of creating. He blessed the creatures and gave them fertility (Genesis 1:22). In his placing of Adam in the garden to serve and protect it, we can discern a commitment to all of creation, including humanity.

Covenant with all creatures after the flood

The first time the word 'covenant' is used in the Bible is in Genesis 6 to 9, the story of the flood. At the end of the flood, the animals spill out of the ark and repopulate the land. In this story, God makes his covenant with the community of creatures: 'I now establish my covenant with you [Noah] and with your descendants after you and with every living creature that was with you' (9:9–10). God makes a commitment in his covenant that he will never again flood the Earth. This covenant is more specific than God's commitment in Genesis 1—2, which was to the whole of creation. It is made specifically with humans and other living creatures: 'the birds, the livestock and all the wild animals' (v. 10). The purpose of the flood had been to wipe away living creatures in response to growing violence (6:13–17), so the covenant may be limited to 'creatures' because this is where violence had been developing, possibly with animals as well as humans. The relationships change (9:2–3): the animals now fear humans (perhaps with good reason, because humans are now allowed to eat them), but Noah is commanded not to eat animals with the life blood still in them (v. 4). This is to acknowledge that all life is a gift and does not belong to humans but to God.

Of all the biblical covenants, this one is often portrayed in the most picturesque terms: we see the ark on the mountain, with the animals spilling out, Noah looking up to God with gratitude, and the rainbow reaching across the scene. The reality, however, is a limitation of violence and a demarcation of relationship boundaries between humans and animals that fall well short of the creation ideal.[31]

Our relationship to the environment today is much more likely to follow this pattern than the more ideal one in Genesis 1—2. So often we lack the honesty to see that our limitation of damage to creation is far short of God's ideal. With climate change, the various summits have sought agreements to limit damage to the climate by restricting carbon emissions. None have sought a more radical path to set measures in place that would eventually return the Earth to its pre-industrial atmospheric composition. Some Christians place hope in God's promise not to flood the Earth again. We must note that the present threat of out-of-control climate change comes from the actions of humans and not God. However, the rainbow is a sign of God's commitment to his creation and points towards his ultimate redemption of the cosmos that he created and loves.

Covenant with Abraham: a link between humans and the land

The next covenant is more specific. The covenant with Abraham is for Abraham and his descendants and is intimately bound up with the land. This covenant is with a specific people and connects them to a specific land. 'The Earth' and 'land' in English are translations of the same word in Hebrew, *eretz*. Thus Abraham is promised descendants who have an ongoing relationship with a specific part of the Earth. There is a strong sense of God's election and of a call to have a relationship with one bit of creation. For me (Margot), leaving home and going to university started me on a journey away from my childhood homeland of Somerset. For many people today, it is easy to feel rootless and to lack connection with the place where we live. Yet in this covenant we can see a principle of God's purposes for us. We each need to work out our life in context, and there is strength to be gained from committing to one place and one people. This will not be the call for everyone but for those who can commit long-term to one community. The resulting rooted relationships will be beneficial to that local bit of Earth as well as to human community. The covenant with Abraham is therefore not out of context with creation but is one where people and creation are yet again connected together.

Covenant with Moses: law and ethical living

The Bible study in chapter 2 gave us some insight into the covenant with Moses. Here, the law is given as a basis of ethical living, and the ten commandments do not concern people alone. The commandment to keep the sabbath includes a rest for animals as well. The Mosaic law also has much to say about crops and other aspects of relating to nature (which will be considered again in chapter 6).

Covenant with David: responsible leadership

The covenant with David was established to develop a concept of just kingly rule (2 Samuel 23:5; 2 Chronicles 13:5; 21:7). It is important to note that the word used when the kings were called by God to 'rule' over his people and land, *radah*, is the same word that is translated as 'dominion' in Genesis 1:26, 28 (NRSV). Our rule of the Earth should be like that of a just king ruling over his nation. One interesting aspect of this covenant is that it is discussed mostly after the death of David, promising that God will not give up on his covenant even though Israel's leaders have not kept it themselves.

Covenant, leadership and environment

As we consider the covenant with leaders, it is important to ask what our modern church leaders have done to enable a just and gentle rule of creation. Many church leaders have made statements about the environment and especially about the need to respond to climate change. Rowan Williams, the former archbishop of Canterbury, sees the cause of climate change in a shared cultural and spiritual crisis, which he describes as 'a loss of a sense of what life is'. He highlights the fact that humanity cannot exist outside ecology. We cannot 'solve' the problem of climate change; we need multifaceted approaches. To be human means to be responsible about the future of life.[32] The present archbishop, Justin Welby, has used his understanding of the corporate world to challenge the investment industry to drive change by pressing companies to meet climate targets and reduce their impact on the environment.[33]

Leadership for creation care in various parts of the worldwide church began to grow in the last decade. The Lausanne Movement made a commitment to caring for God's Earth in their global gathering of church leaders in Cape Town in 2010. Following this, a new creation-care branch of Lausanne was forged in Jamaica in 2012 at a gathering specifically focused on the environment. It has since held regional meetings widely around the world. In Africa there has been a growing movement of 'Green Anglicans', and in 2016 an international meeting in Lusaka had a significant focus on the impact of climate change on the global south and the need for church leaders to respond. In June 2015, Pope Francis published an encyclical on the environment.[34] *Laudato Si'* was timely as the major Paris climate change meeting approached and has had a huge influence on the church and wider society in many parts of the world.

By the start of 2020, we were following a packed schedule as we sought to support a major shift by churches and church leaders to take action on climate change. Our move had proved well-timed, and we supported the launch of the archbishop of Canterbury's Lent Book, *Saying Yes to Life* by Ruth Valerio, and initiatives in Oxford and Bristol Anglican Dioceses and elsewhere. As the pandemic rolled in, it was encouraging to hear national church leaders call to 'build back better' in summer 2020 and Tearfund launched their 'Reboot' campaign.[35] The next few years are vital for safeguarding our climate, and we are hopeful that there will be strong leadership from church leaders, both within the church and as a prophetic voice in the wider world.

Covenant between people, creatures and the Earth

The covenants we have looked at so far are between God and creation or some part of it. We have seen how such covenants are made between a senior and a junior partner and represent a gift to the latter. There is another type of covenant, which is made between two equals, but is brokered by a more senior third party. We see this sort of covenant in Hosea 2:18–23, where God makes a covenant between humans and 'the beasts of the field and the birds of the air and the creatures that move along the ground'. The language is that of betrothal and, as God reconnects people with the Earth, the Earth will respond with fruitfulness. So this covenant is with creatures and also with the Earth itself. It is only through this re-engagement that we will have any hope of regaining the environmental balance that is essential for human survival. Pope Francis wrote in *Laudato Si'*:

> So what they [Christians] all need is an 'ecological conversion', whereby the effects of their encounter with Jesus Christ become evident in their relationship with the world around them. Living our vocation to be protectors of God's handiwork is essential to a life of virtue; it is not an optional or a secondary aspect of our Christian experience.[36]

New covenant in Jeremiah: writing the law on our hearts

The covenant in Jeremiah 31:23–40 takes the ethical law one step further by declaring a covenant where the law will be written on the hearts of the people. As the world began to change, the exiled people of Israel no longer had their historic relationship with their land or temple. The statutes of their ancestors needed to become principles that could be worked out in a fresh setting. We have seen that the written law included many decrees about caring for the Earth, and these are now taken one step further. By writing the law on our hearts, God moves the emphasis from specific statutes to values and principles.

We are now in a new and unknown setting. Humanity has not previously had such a major impact on the planet that we have threatened the survival of a significant portion of the human population and many other species. What does the 'law on our hearts' look like in this context?

The new covenant in Jesus

The new covenant on our hearts in Jeremiah points towards the new covenant in Jesus, who won salvation for us through his willing death on the cross and his resurrection, defeating death. We will explore the implications of this covenant more fully in later chapters. It is important to note here that this covenant does not abolish the previous covenants but is the culmination of them.[37] In Jeremiah, the Hebrew word for 'new' is *hadashah*. This implies not 'brand new' but 'repaired or 'renewed' (see Isaiah 61:4; 1 Samuel 11:14). Likewise, one Greek word for new is *kainos* and this is used for new creation in Revelation 21. Kainos does not usually mean 'brand new', which is *neos* in Greek. *Kainos* implies a renewing and remaking of the old. God is into recycling!

Each of the covenants represents some aspect of God's relationship with his creation and of the interconnection between people and the Earth. The new covenant is the final fulfilment and points towards the ultimate restoration of those relationships at the end of time (Revelation 21 to 22). We will then find ourselves in perfect covenant unity that will lead to peace and well-being for all.

Living in covenant

We have traced the theme of covenant through the Bible and can see that it is a key concept to enable us to reconnect with God, creation and each other. Hosea's covenant was brokered by God to enable humans and the Earth to reconnect in a relationship of well-being. In the face of climate change it is time to ask for God's help once again to renew our relationship with the Earth.

ECOTIP We've been to many talks on climate change, where, after the seriousness of the situation has been presented, the advised response has been to change our light bulbs! The sheer size of the problem can overwhelm any response we might make. Though many changes seem insignificant, they do make a huge difference if everyone does them, and the impact of changing to energy-efficient appliances can already be measured. Insulating your home, switching to green energy, walking and cycling more and, if you have a car, getting a fully electric one when you next need to change are all things that really will make a difference. Beyond that, our ECOtip for climate change is to get active. You might like to write to your MP, local councillors or other political representatives. There are many online petitions. There are also climate marches, campaigns and events. If there is to be real action for this most serious of problems, our politicians need to know that we care.

Bible study: living lives that declare the glory of God

We sometimes talk about the 'laws of nature', and this reflects our experience that nature is wonderfully crafted with complex mathematics and intricate patterns running through the physical and biological world. In our desire to have wealth, comfort and mobility, we have taken too much from nature and added dangerous pollutants to it. As our climate shifts in response we find ourselves in a more unstable and unpredictable world. How do we live lives that declare the glory of God?

Read Psalm 19

1 What are the glories of God's creation that you value?
2 When you see nature in all its glory, how do you feel and what is your response to God?
3 In what ways have you ignored God's precepts in our use of the world's resources?
4 In verse 12, the psalmist admits that he did not realise he was doing wrong. How does that apply to our generation?
5 What might be 'ruling over us' that we might need to change?
6 The psalm ends by reminding us that God is our Rock and our Redeemer. Spend time in prayer at the end of the study and remind each other of these words.

Notes

1   A Rocha has uploaded videos and resources from this tour at **atyourservice.arocha.org/en/hope-for-planet-earth-2009-resource-pack** (accessed 15 July 2020).
2   Intergovernmental Panel on Climate Change (IPCC), **ipcc.ch** (accessed 24 July 2020).
3   *Chasing Ice* (Exposure, 2012), **chasingice.com** (accessed 27 September 2020).
4   L.M. Lombrana, A. Shiryaevskaya, D. Khrennikova, O. Tanas and M. Rojanasakul, 'A front-row seat for the Arctic's final summers with ice', *Bloomberg Green*, 27 July 2020, **bloomberg.com/graphics/2020-arctic-sea-ice-crossing** (accessed 28 July 2020).
5   R.S. Nerem, B.D. Beckley, J.T. Fasullo, B.D. Hamlington, D. Masters and G.T. Mitchum, 'Climate-change-driven accelerated sea-level rise detected in the altimeter era', *PNAS* 115 (2018), pp. 2022–25, **doi.org/10.1073/pnas.1717312115**.
6   R. Pidcock, R. Pearce and R. McSweeney, 'Mapped: How climate change affects extreme weather around the world', *CarbonBrief*, 15 April 2020, **carbonbrief.org/mapped-how-climate-change-affects-extreme-weather-around-the-world** (accessed 20 July 2020).
7   J.P. Kossin et al., 'Global increase in major tropical cyclone exceedance probability over the past four decades', *PNAS* 117, no. 22 (2020), pp. 11975–980, **doi.org/10.1073/pnas.1920849117**.
8   J.B. Elsner, T. Fricker and Z. Schroder, 'Increasingly powerful tornadoes in the United States', *Geophysical Research Letters*, 46 (2019), pp. 392–98, **doi.org/10.1029/2018GL080819**.
9   P. Ghosh, 'Climate change boosted Australia bushfire risk by at least 30%', *BBC News*, 4 March 2020, **bbc.co.uk/news/science-environment-51742646** (accessed 30 July 2020).
10 Typhoons and hurricanes are essentially the same, but the former happen in the Pacific Ocean while hurricanes occur in the Atlantic Ocean.
11 'Super Typhoon Haiyan', *CIMSS Satellite Blog*, 7 November 2013, **cimss.ssec.wisc.edu/satellite-blog/archives/14311** (accessed 4 September 2020).
12 In 2016 Margot oversaw a major pastoral reorganisation and Haddenham Benefice merged with another to form the Wychert Vale Benefice.

13 Haddenham in Transition later morphed into Zero Carbon Haddenham, **zeroch.org** (accessed 15 July 2020).

14 *The Age of Stupid* (Spanner Films, 2009), **spannerfilms.net/films/ ageofstupid** (accessed 15 July 2020).

15 We discussed this incident and the whole topic of climate scepticism in M.J. Hodson and M.R. Hodson, *The Ethics of Climatic Scepticism* (Grove Booklets, 2015).

16 M.J. Hodson, 'Paris, Paris-COP 21, a personal reflection and review', *Special JRI Briefing*, 13 December 2015, **jri.org.uk/paris2015** (accessed 12 February 2021).

17 See Briefings 32 and 34 at **jri.org.uk/briefings** (accessed 31 July 2020).

18 R. Valerio et al., *Covid-19*.

19 C. Le Quéré et al., 'Temporary reduction in daily global CO_2 emissions during the Covid-19 forced confinement', *Nature Climate Change* 10 (2020), pp. 647–53, **doi.org/10.1038/s41558-020-0797-x** (accessed 31 July 2020).

20 J. Houghton, 'Why care for the environment?' in D. Alexander (ed.), *Has Science Killed God?* (SPCK, 2019), pp. 238–50.

21 M.J. Hodson, 'Sir John Houghton (1931–2020)', *JRI* , 16 April 2020, **jri.org.uk/news/sir-john-houghton-1931-2020** (accessed 3 August 2020).

22 For a report on where we stood on the 20 January 2021, see M.J. Hodson, 'Biden inauguration day: what next for the environment?' *JRI* , **jri.org.uk/blog/biden-inauguration-day-what-next-for-the-environment**. Regular updates on the run up to COP26 and its aftermath can be found at **jri.org.uk** (both accessed 23 January 2021).

23 For a good account of tipping points, see Lynas, *The God Species*, pp. 60–64.

24 IPCC, 'Global warming of 1.5°C', **ipcc.ch/sr15** (accessed 3 August 2020).

25 N. Myers, 'Environmental refugees: a growing phenomenon of the 21st century', *Philosophical Transactions of the Royal Society, London*, B 357 (2002), pp. 609–13.

26 A.M. Findlay, 'Migrant destinations in an era of environmental change', *Global Environmental Change* 21 (2011), **doi.org/10.1016/j. gloenvcha.2011.09.004**.

27   G.J. Abel, M. Brottrager, J. Crespo Cuaresma, and R. Muttarakd, 'Climate, conflict and forced migration', *Global Environmental Change* 54 (2019), **doi.org/10.1016/J.GLOENVCHA.2018.12.003**.

28   N. Oreskes and E.M. Conway, *The Collapse of Western Civilization: A view from the future* (Columbia University Press, 2014).

29   G. von Rad, *Old Testament Theology*, volume 1 (SCM, 1975), p. 129.

30   D.L. Clough, *On Animals: Systematic Theology* (T&T Clarke, 2012), p. 16.

31   Bauckham, *Bible and Ecology*, pp. 23–25.

32   R. Williams, 'The climate crisis: fashioning a Christian response', lecture at Southwark Cathedral, sponsored by Operation Noah, 13 October 2009, **youtube.com/watch?v=rHAkJLUHxmE** (accessed 8 January 2021).

33   S. Farrell, 'Justin Welby: investors must pressure firms to act on climate crisis', *The Guardian*, 27 August 2019, **theguardian.com/uk-news/2019/aug/27/justin-welby-investors-must-pressure-firms-act-climate-crisis** (accessed 5 September 2020)

34   A papal encyclical is an extended letter containing an important message, usually addressed to Catholic Church leaders. This encyclical is addressed to 'every person living on this planet'. It contains a powerful message urging everyone to respond to the environmental crisis. The Pope especially challenged world leaders and the wealthy west. The document can be viewed at **laudatosi.org/pope-francis/encyclical-letter** (accessed 3 August 2020).

35   Tearfund Reboot campaign, **tearfund.org/campaigns/reboot-campaign** (accessed 5 August 2020).

36   *Laudato Si'*, 217. For a detailed appraisal of the idea of 'ecological conversion' see T. Howles, J. Reader and M.J. Hodson, 'Creating an ecological citizenship': philosophical and theological perspectives on the role of contemporary environmental education', *The Heythrop Journal* 59 (2018), pp. 997–1008, **doi.org/10.1111/heyj.13015**.

37   D. Bookless, *The Bible and Biodiversity* (Jubilee Centre Cambridge Paper, October 2014), **jubilee-centre.org/cambridge-papers/bible-and-biodiversity** (accessed 5 August 2020).

4 WATER

Both sides of the mountain

In autumn 2012 we first visited the Alpujarras area on the southern flank of the Sierra Nevada mountain range in Spain. The area has had a turbulent history, with both Christian and Muslim (Moorish) rulers. The Moors ruled Andalucía from AD711 (when they invaded from North Africa) to 1492, with the fall of Granada. They were great builders and experts in irrigation systems, which were much needed to increase agricultural production for a growing population. One day, as we walked north of the village of Capileira, we had a great view of the Moorish terraces cut into the sides of the mountains, still evident today. We later found ourselves lost on another walk and followed one of the ancient channels (*acequias*) to find our way back. When the Moors were finally expelled from the Alpujarras in 1568, a few families were allowed to stay in each village to look after the irrigation systems.

Water is still a very important issue in southern Spain. The summer of 2012 brought Spain its worst drought in 70 years. We visited the Jardin de la Alpujarra,[1] not far from Pitres, where we were staying. There, two Englishmen, Robert and William, had set up a small gar-den some eight years previously. At 1,250 metres above sea level, it is not the easiest location for garden-ing. The temperature ranges from below freezing in the winter, when it frequently snows, to the low 30s cen-tigrade in the summer months. All had gone well with the garden until summer 2012, when the extended

drought meant that water was totally cut off for irrigation from July, and quite a number of the plants in the garden died. William showed us around the gardens and told us of their plans to switch focus away from plants that required irrigation. With drier weather expected in the future, the new aim was to plant species that could cope with drought.

We returned to the garden on our sabbatical trip in 2014, and, after two less severe years, the garden was looking a lot better. Robert explained that they had now planted some more drought-tolerant species. Their water came along *acequias* from Trevelez, and they were near the end of the line. So, although 2014 was not a bad year for rain, by the end of the summer in September their *acequia* was quite dry. This was in total contrast to Los Olivos, a retreat centre near Lecrin, twelve miles on the other side of the mountain, where we stayed earlier in the trip. There we were told that they have ample water every year and were not affected even by the drought in 2012, so a relatively short distance can make all the difference to how restricted the water supply is.

On our last visit to the garden in May 2017, Robert and William invited Martin to give a talk to an enthusiastic group of local gardeners, 'How garden plants tolerate a hot, dry climate'. Gardening in an environment where water is often in short supply is never easy.

Water: a global perspective

We live on a planet that is dominated by water. Over 70 per cent of the Earth's surface is covered by oceans and, viewed from space, the dominant colour is blue, not green. So it is slightly ironic that water is such a problem for humanity.[2] The snag, of course, is that the oceans are salt water, which means 97.5 per cent of the water in the world is not suitable for us to drink or to use for watering our crops. Salt water can be used once it has passed through a desalination plant, but the process is expensive and most plants run on fossil fuels, contributing to the increase in greenhouse gases. In 2019 the 16,000 desalination plants worldwide supplied only about 0.5 per cent of the global water demand. These plants are very useful in areas where there is almost no fresh water (such as Arabia), but they cannot provide a solution to global fresh water shortages. Of the 2.5 per cent of water that is not saline, most is locked up in ice caps and glaciers, at least at the moment (see chapter 3). Only about 0.01 per cent of the Earth's water is the liquid in our streams, rivers and lakes. The problem is that the amount of available fresh water is the same now as it was at the time of Jesus, 2,000 years ago, but in that time the world human population has increased from about 250 million to 7.8 billion (see chapter 5). We also have many more water-hungry processes than we did 2,000 years ago.

Water continually moves through the hydrological cycle and about 110,000 km^3 of water falls as rain, sleet and snow each year. Of that, the majority (64 per cent) returns to the atmosphere through evaporation and evapotranspiration (where water passes through plants and is lost from the leaves). The remainder forms the runoff that goes into our streams, rivers, lakes and underground aquifers, and eventually makes its way to the sea. At least, it would eventually make it to the sea if humans did not intervene. We use that water as drinking water, to irrigate our crops, in hydroelectric schemes and in industrial processes.

Humans have been very successful at controlling rivers. In 1950 there were about 5,000 large dams, but there are now over 58,000. These dams control a sizeable amount of the runoff water and, in many cases, rivers never reach the sea. This is the case with the Colorado River: now, 40 per cent of the water supplied to Phoenix, Arizona, comes from this river. The decreased flow, downstream of dams, is extremely bad news for the fish and other wildlife living in the rivers or relying on them. Even when flow is maintained, it may not vary in a 'natural' way, and dams often take out much of the sediment from rivers, endangering deltas that rely on continued input of sediment. Perhaps the worst example of water extraction from rivers causing environmental problems is the Aral Sea in Central Asia. This was once the fourth largest lake in the world, but, following the diversion of the rivers that fed it to supply cotton fields, it shrank to a fraction of its former volume and became a major ecological disaster.

Postel defines fresh water sustainability as follows:

> In any watershed, ensure that basic water needs are met for all people; preserve ecological infrastructure so as to provide the quantity, quality, and timing of water flows needed to sustain ecosystem services; and where groundwater is tapped, ensure extraction does not deplete the water in storage or degrade connected ecosystems.[3]

Really good progress has been made on the first clause, and in the last 25 years many more people have been enabled to have access safe drinking water, but 2.2 billion people in 2017 still did not have this access (see chapter 9). Proper sanitation is still a major need. But we are undoubtedly failing badly with clauses two and three. Dams are seriously affecting the ecology of freshwater systems and many aquifers are being extracted too quickly. We can conclude that our use of water is currently not sustainable.

Water in Spain

Spain is mostly a fairly arid country, and during our sabbatical visit we decided to investigate water and how it is managed there. On our way down from Alcala near Madrid to the Sierra Nevada in the south, we needed a stopping place for a few days halfway. Margot found just what we were looking for in Ruidera. As we drove there in late August, it was predictably hot and the land was parched after the summer, but when we arrived in Ruidera we entered a totally different world. The Lagunas de Ruidera are a series of 15 lakes, inter-connected by streams and waterfalls. This whole area, La Mancha, is the land of the fictional anti-hero Don Quixote, and there is a walking trail named after him that passes near Ruidera. Miguel de Cervantes mentions the lakes in *Don Quixote*, but he mentions only seven. The lakes are a vivid blue colour because of high calcium carbonate content, which has precipitated out over thousands of years to form the tufa deposits that line the lakes and form the waterfalls.[4] As we approached the largest waterfall, El Hundimiento, a crayfish wandered across our path. Crayfish normally live underwater but can survive out of water for a short time. He looked a bit worried as we approached, and we later found out that he is considered a delicacy by the Spanish!

Ruidera is an exceptional oasis in an otherwise dry land. Spain, with its Mediterranean climate, has distinct rainy and dry seasons. Such areas have been subject to considerable water infrastructure development, as conservation of water for the dry season is very important. Let us take, for example, the River Ebro, the longest in Spain.[5] The river flows 930 km from the mountains south of Santander to the Mediterranean, some 160 km south of Barcelona. Within the river basin there are two large cities, Zaragoza and Pamplona, but the dominant land use is for agriculture and 10 per cent of the basin is irrigated land. There are 289 dams on the river, which collect over 50 per cent of the mean annual runoff, and 340 hydroelectric facilities. Many of the dams were constructed during the time of the Franco dictatorship, leaving Spain with one of the greatest densities of dams in the world. Agriculture became more intensive during that time, and that led to water pollution problems from fertilisers and pesticides. Spanish water policy later came to be influenced by the European Union, particularly through the Water Framework Directive. This brought in a far more holistic approach, which incorporated aquatic ecosystem protection. Even now, however, the problems of water scarcity, pollution and overexploitation have not been entirely solved.

What of the future? We saw in chapter 3 that climate change will have big effects globally, but what is likely to happen in Spain and how will this affect Spanish water resources?[6] Between 1950 and 2002, many parts of the Iberian Peninsula showed decreased precipitation of at least 50 mm per annum, but the north-west showed an increase. Comparing the Mediterranean region for the period 1960–1990 with 2040–2070, a temperature increase of 2°C to 3°C is projected.

Annual precipitation is likely to show a marked decrease across most of the Mediterranean basin. The south of Spain is likely to be badly affected, with a decrease of around 15 per cent expected. Northern Spain, however, is likely to only show a slight decrease. Temperature and precipitation changes of this order are likely to affect snow accumulation and melting processes in mountain ranges such as the Sierra Nevada in southern Spain. Reduced groundwater recharge into aquifers of around 16 per cent is predicted in Spain by the middle of this century. Clearly, these changes will put enormous pressure on already stretched water resources in Spain. This will call for considerable improvements in water management, particularly in the south and east of the country. In a recent study of the Segura River Basin in south-east Spain, Morote and his colleagues investigated the use of non-conventional water resources (desalination and water reuse).[7] Their conclusion was that the integration of these resources had allowed one of the driest areas in Spain to become highly resilient to drought, and to prepare for future changes in the climate.

Too much water: floods

Most of this chapter concerns the problems of too little water, and this is a big issue globally, but there are times when we get too much water, which can lead to serious flooding. We asked Rob Walrond, a farmer and the rural officer for Bath and Wells diocese in the UK, to explain the impact of the floods on the Somerset Levels from 2012 to 2014. This is his account:

> The Somerset Levels are an area of predominantly pastureland which for centuries have been drained and managed by man-made waterways. They will flood in times of high rainfall, with the water being removed by a series of pumps and sluices. Livestock farming (mainly beef cattle) predominates in this area, with some dairy farming and lamb production. Unseasonably high rainfall between spring 2012 and winter 2013–14 led to an increased frequency and severity of flooding events. Flooding

during spring/summer 2012 caused damage to thousands of hectares of pastureland, where grass and arable crops literally rotted in the fields. Subsequent reseeding and pasture repair was destroyed by repeated flooding during winter 2013–14. The severity of this flooding was such that over 12,000 hectares were flooded at depths of up to three metres. Over 200 homes were flooded and twelve farms had to be evacuated, with over 1,000 cattle and 250 sheep having to be moved to other farms. In all, over 200 farms were affected, with some land flooded for in excess of 13 weeks.

The Farming Community Network (FCN)[8] has supported a number of farming families on the Levels, with significant fear concerning the viability of farming on the Levels in the future. The quality of grazing on the Levels has deteriorated markedly in recent years, partly due to environmental pressure to maintain high water levels for the benefit of bird and insect life. A significant proportion of land has been purchased by conservation and wildlife groups. Farmers are increasingly unable to follow the agricultural practices that helped this area become such a vibrant wildlife haven, and they also feel that the ability of this area to produce food is rapidly diminishing.

The speed and frequency of flooding are becoming a greater concern, and this has been exacerbated by increased building on flood plains and flood-prevention work upstream. The Levels are now routinely used as a sacrifice area or water-storage area to safeguard urban developments. Farmers may need to be paid to store water on their land rather than use it to produce food.

Biblical reflection: Water and salvation

Jerusalem and water

We have seen that Spain has a long history of coping with a dry climate. This has also been true of Israel, and the Bible has many texts relating to water.

Jerusalem has always been a very dry city. Chosen as a defensive site, its key point of vulnerability was its lack of water.[9] The Gihon Spring was the nearest natural water source but was outside the city, in the Kidron Valley. In ancient times, a simple shaft was built to reach the spring, giving apparent security but also proving to be a point of weakness. King David used the shaft to enter the city and conquer it (2 Samuel 5:6–8). Later, King Hezekiah built a second, more sophisticated tunnel to take the water from the spring to a pool called Siloam (2 Kings 20:20). Here it could be stored within the city and reached in relative safety. It is still possible to visit Hezekiah's Tunnel. You find yourself transported through the centuries as you walk through the dark, narrow tunnel. Do take a torch and expect to get wet!

In New Testament times there was a special ceremony during the autumn festival of Tabernacles, when the city was filled with booths, decked with fruit. The priests would go daily to the Pool of Siloam and draw water, returning to the temple singing the 'Hallel' Psalms. The water was poured on the altar with prayers for rain after the long dry summer. On the last day of the feast there would be a special prayer for rain and salvation. On this day Jesus said, 'Let anyone who is thirsty come to me and drink. Whoever believes in me, as Scripture has said, rivers of living water will flow from within them' (John 7:37–38). Reading these words in context, we understand their impact. Jesus promises salvation to all who follow him, using an image central to the spiritual and environmental understanding of his hearers. Amid prayers for physical rain and salvation, Jesus offers living water.

This promise culminates in the outpouring of salvation in the future Jerusalem. In Revelation 22, dry Jerusalem becomes the source of the river of life, emanating from God's throne. The water flows through the streets of the human world and then out to water the natural world. Here the tree of life produces fruit and leaves that will, in turn, heal the nations. It is a picture of perfect harmony between God, people and creation. This is the final culmination of the covenant.

Finding living water

'The sun is shining!' In July 2020, we were recording interviews to put in our online benefice service, broadcast each week during the pandemic. John Eustace, a local farmer and churchwarden, had already had Margot dressed up in bee-keeping kit to find out what was under the roof of a beehive (Martin stayed at a safe distance, filming). Now John had invited us to come and film a new artesian well that he had been drilling with an enormous drill built into a large lorry. The well was for two new cottages that had been built 'off grid' and needed their own supply of water.

The borehole was in deep shade – hence the need for sunshine. When we arrived, John took the cap off the top of the well. Water was pouring out from beneath the metal plate, and it would have been easy to become soaked. John explained about the geology and how he had been able to tell that this location would be a good one to find water. We were just south of the Cotswold hills, and the cottages were in a perfect position to be able to drill down to water that would come up under its own pressure.

We filmed John skilfully capping the wellhead again and talked about water in the Bible and Jesus as the water of life. We decided to make this the focus of our service for that week, and, as well as online, we held a wonderful open-air service in the grounds of Alvescot church, gathering people from all over our benefice. In the depths of the pandemic it was good to give thanks for the gift of water for drinking, cleansing and watering our crops. More than all of these, we were thankful for Jesus, the water of life, who was sustaining us through such a tough time by giving us streams of living water. It was one of the most joyful services we can remember.

Salvation, water and creation

Water and salvation have long been connected. When Moses brought the people out of Egypt, he 'saved' them by taking them through the sea (Exodus 14:29–30). The salvation imagery in Isaiah is closely linked to water: for example, 'With joy you will draw water from the wells of salvation' (12:3), and later, 'You heavens above, rain down my righteousness; let the clouds shower it down. Let the earth open wide, let salvation spring up' (45:8). In Isaiah, too, the awfulness of people's rejection of God is portrayed with images of drought and famine ('The earth dries up and withers', 24:4), but when they turn back to God, it will be like the rains coming: 'I, the God of Israel, will not forsake them. I will make rivers flow on barren heights' (41:17–18). In the dry Middle East, this imagery is powerful. Hearers of Isaiah's prophecies were only too aware of the suffering caused by drought, and of the blessing of abundant water. These images give a vivid picture of God's salvation promise.[10] Jeremiah uses the same imagery to announce judgement: 'My people... have forsaken me, the spring of living water, and have dug their own cisterns, broken cisterns that cannot hold water' (Jeremiah 2:13). Flowing water is described as 'living' in the Bible, and it is seen as more valuable than stored cistern water. All these images draw on the blessings and curses in Deuteronomy 28, where God blesses with 'rain on your land in season' (v. 12) and will judge his people by turning the rain into dust (v. 24).

Here is an important environmental message: when humans disregard the God-given limits of the Earth, there are serious ecological consequences. The Aral Sea (mentioned above) is a good example. There is also a spiritual message that goes beyond the usual horizons of Christian understanding. Many parts of the Bible portray future salvation as being not just for humans; there is also salvation for creation. In Isaiah, this idea is portrayed initially as a restoration of *shalom* (peace and well-being) for the whole creation. We see it in Isaiah 11:6–9, where the wolf lives with the lamb and 'the earth will be filled with the knowledge of the Lord as the waters cover the sea'. This image promises salvation framed as a restoration of covenant (see chapter 3), in which peace and well-being were among the purposes of the covenant. Relationships in a restored covenant are characterised by trust. The Earth is filled with God's wisdom. The second aspect of salvation in Isaiah is the ultimate renewal of creation. In Isaiah 65:17–25, God declares a renewed heaven and Earth, where there will be an end to suffering, a restoration of peace, and agricultural harmony between humans and creation. This is a far cry from a return to pristine wilderness, although there is a promise for wild animals and uncultivated places, in Isaiah 43:20: 'The wild animals honour me, the jackals and the owls, because I provide water in the wilderness and streams in the wasteland.' Once again, the salvation imagery includes water.

So how can we understand salvation for creation alongside humanity? Many Christian environmental thinkers have investigated Romans 8:18–26,[11] where creation is described as groaning, waiting for glory, and subjected to frustration with the hope of being liberated. Some make the case that salvation is primarily for humans but that God has a secondary interest in salvation for creation.[12] Their argument is based on the observation that 'the sons of God' seem central to the passage. Animal ethicist David Clough argues against this peripheral view. He sees human redemption as vital but feels that it is dangerous to jump to the claim that creation is only of secondary importance.[13] Richard Bauckham perceives the destiny of humans and the rest of creation as bound up together: 'If there is hope for the people, then there must also be hope for the non-human creation.'[14]

The images of water in the Bible remind us of our dependence on the Earth and how deeply we are bound together. In the passages about a future restoration of creation, we see the hand of a loving God who will renew his creation beyond our wildest dreams. We understand our place in creation as one of awesome responsibility to lead wisely. One day, that role will be fulfilled, when we will lead a redeemed creation as a redeemed people of God.

Christian Engineers in Development

In the words of a UN resolution, 'Water is critical for sustainable development, including environmental integrity and the alleviation of poverty and hunger, and is indispensable for human health and well-being.'[15]

As Christians we are called to point towards salvation, and we can see an example of this in the work of Christian Engineers in Development (CED). We asked Barbara Brighouse, the CED company secretary, to tell us about their work:

> CED is a membership organisation for engineers seeking to use their practical skills to serve communities in the majority world. Members give their time voluntarily, and we have no office, so overheads are minimal. Projects we have assisted with over the last 30+ years have been wide-ranging, but the most common request, by far, is for water supplies.[16]
>
> The challenge this presents is becoming greater as climate change affects rainfall patterns, making flood and drought events more common and previously reliable water sources inadequate. The benefits of rainwater harvesting (RWH), while not a complete solution, are increasingly being realised by rural communities, and part of CED's work is to run courses in RWH systems, including ferro-cement tank construction. A key aim is to enable competent local trainees to become trainers themselves, in accordance with our aim of 'sharing skills, changing lives'.
>
> The best solution to a community's water-supply issue is one that will have a reliable yield and be easy to maintain. In any project, a competent local partner organisation is essential, as is community involvement at all stages. Our part includes the design, help with accessing funding and general oversight of the work. Day-to-day supervision and ongoing support are done by our partners, as we do not have a continued presence in any project countries.

Whatever the source, the benefits of readily available, safe water are far-reaching. Improved health and much-reduced time spent collecting water create income-generating potential, and mothers are better able to care for their children. School attendance is improved, and teachers are easier to employ. Anxiety is reduced, family relationships improve and girls are less susceptible to rape while collecting water. Households must pay a maintenance levy, but they spend less on medicines. Water brings life and, where possible and with God's grace, we will continue to assist in bringing it to those in need.[17]

Jesus, salvation and the cross

At the heart of salvation is the cross and Jesus' suffering to bring salvation to the world. Jesus promised living water to all who followed him, but poignantly, as he was dying, he said, 'I am thirsty.' After he had received a drink of wine vinegar, he gave up his spirit. Later a soldier pierced his side and blood and water flowed out (John 19:28–37). Jesus, source of the living water of life, was drained of physical water. This is a powerful reminder of the cost of salvation, willingly given because God so loved his cosmos (John 3:16). The awfulness of the cross leads to the astonishing gift of salvation. Jesus' sacrifice was sufficient for salvation for the whole of creation, and we are called to work out that salvation in our relationships not only with other people but also with the natural world.

 ECOTIP **Bottled water has become very fashionable and 'feels' very healthy. However, it takes energy and oil to make the bottles, process the water and transport it, sometimes thousands of miles, to be sold in shops. If you like bottled water, you could try investing in a machine to purify your own water – or you might simply use water from the tap!**

Bible study: salvation for people and creation

One morning we took a walk through the beautiful Alpujarra Mountains. We started with the moon still visible as we walked through the whitewashed medieval village. As we climbed on to the hill, the sun was coming up and the colours of the mountains changed in a kaleidoscope of light as the morning gathered strength. As we returned we saw a pair of majestic Booted Eagles rising on the thermals in the valley.

The poetic language of Isaiah helps us understand more fully the salvation of God in relation to people and the rest of creation.

Read Isaiah 55:6–13

1 What sort of landscape does Isaiah describe in this passage and why is rain so important to it?
2 How is rain perceived in your community? Do you have too much or too little? Is it valued enough?
3 Isaiah compares rain watering the Earth to the word of God going forth into the world. How does this relate to the call to 'seek the Lord'?
4 The effect of the rain is to make the Earth 'bud and flourish', and one of the crops is grain that is made into bread. This reminds us that the bread and wine of Communion are the 'fruit of the Earth'. What are the implications for the way we understand Christ and creation?
5 In the Middle East, reconciliation between two formerly divided parties was forged by having a fellowship meal together. This meal would always involve bread and wine. In what ways can we remember and demonstrate the reconciled relationships between ourselves, God, other humans and creation?
6 The final section of the passage looks towards the joy of God's creation restored and reconciled. Plants symbolic of a damaged creation (briers and thorns) are replaced by those associated

with fruitfulness (myrtle and pine). It is here that we have the wonderful image of trees clapping their hands (see the Prologue to this book). In what ways can we express the joy of creation in our personal lives and in church?

Notes

1 Jardin de la Alpujarra, **jardinalpujarra.com** (accessed 6 August 2020).

2 In this section we have drawn on the following sources: M.J. Hodson, 'Losing hope? The environmental crisis today', *Anvil* 29 (2013), pp. 7–23; Lynas, *The God Species*, pp. 139–151; S. Postel, 'Sustaining freshwater and its dependents', in Worldwatch Institute (eds), *State of the World 2013: Is sustainability still possible?* , Kindle edition (Island Press, 2013), ch. 5.

3 Postel, 'Sustaining freshwater and its dependents'.

4 S. Ordonez, J.A. Gonzalez Martın, M.A. Garcıa del Cura and H.M. Pedley, 'Temperate and semi-arid tufas in the Pleistocene to recent fluvial barrage system in the Mediterranean area: the Ruidera Lakes Natural Park (central Spain)', *Geomorphology* 69 (2005), pp. 332–50.

5 T.E. Grantham, R. Figueroa and N. Prat, 'Water management in Mediterranean river basins: a comparison of management frameworks, physical impacts, and ecological responses', *Hydrobiologia* 719 (2012), pp. 451–82.

6 J.M. García-Ruiz, J.I. López-Moreno, S.M. Vicente-Serrano, T. Lasanta-Martínez and S. Beguería, 'Mediterranean water resources in a global change scenario', *Earth-Science Reviews* 105 (2011), pp. 121–39.

7 Á.F. Morote, J. Olcina and M. Hernández, 'The use of non-conventional water resources as a means of adaptation to drought and climate change in semi-arid regions: south-eastern Spain', *Water* 11 (2019), 93, **doi.org/10.3390/w11010093**.

8 The Farming Community Network (FCN), **fcn.org.uk** (accessed 3 July 2020).

9 M.R. Hodson, *A Feast of Seasons* (Monarch, 2000), pp. 125ff.

10 M.R. Hodson, *Understanding Isaiah's Environmental Ethics* (Grove Publications, 2011).

11 For example, Bauckham, *Bible and Ecology*, pp. 95–101; D.L. Clough, *On Animals: Volume 1: Systematic Theology* (Bloomsbury, 2012), p. xvii n.21; Hodson and Hodson, *Cherishing the Earth*, pp. 75–78.

12 C.L. Hunt, D. Horrell and C. Southgate, 'An environmental mantra? Ecological interest in Romans 8:19–23 and a modest proposal for a narrative interpretation', *Journal of Theological Studies* 59 (2008), pp. 546–79.

13 Clough, *On Animals*, p. xviii.

14 Bauckham, *Bible and Ecology*, p. 99.

15 UN, Resolution adopted by the General Assembly: '58/217. International Decade for Action, "Water for Life", 2005–2015' (2003), **un-documents.net/a58r217.htm** (accessed 24 August 2020).

16 To learn more about the effects of water, sanitation and hygiene, see **unwater.org/water-facts/water-sanitation-and-hygiene** (accessed 6 July 2020).

17 For more information on the work of CED, see **ced.org.uk** (accessed 6 July 2020).

5 HUMAN POPULATION AND CONSUMPTION

Beijing

In September 2011, I (Martin) visited Beijing, as I had been invited to speak at the fifth 'Silicon in Agriculture' conference there. I had worked on silicon and plants for over 30 years, and it was good to meet up with many old friends. I had one day in the city before the conference began, and I decided to take the underground train from my hotel down to the centre. There I visited two of Beijing's sights, the Forbidden City and Tiananmen Square. The Forbidden City complex consists of 980 buildings, erected between 1406 and 1420, which formed the Chinese imperial palace from the Ming dynasty to the end of the Qing dynasty. When these impressive structures were built, the Chinese human population stood at about 89 million[1] and the old city of Beijing occupied 62 km². Tiananmen Square is the largest square in Beijing and is just to the south of the Forbidden City. It is most famous to us as the scene of pro-democracy protests in 1989, in which many protestors were shot. One brave unknown man attempted to halt a column of tanks just by standing in front of them. Nobody knows what happened to him.

When I walked across Tiananmen Square in 2011, there were about 1,344 million people in China, over 15 times the number when the Forbidden City was built. The area of Beijing is now more than ten times bigger than in imperial times, at about 750 km^2. I was fortunate in that the weather conditions in Beijing at the time were keeping the worst of the smog away, but air pollution in the city is very real. In January 2014, the problem became so bad that the sunrise was televised on giant TV screens in the Square;[2] people there would otherwise never see it. Air pollution levels in Chinese cities have remained high, although there was a temporary decrease when the country was under lockdown during the early part of 2020, due to the Covid-19 pandemic.

I was staying in the Beijing Friendship Hotel, and traffic in the area was heavy. As recently as the 1980s most people cycled to work, but now the car is dominant, and journeys around the city often take a very long time through clogged streets. The hotel was huge and several large conferences were running at the same time. I was pleased to see that, in the building opposite ours, they were holding a workshop on measures to reduce greenhouse emissions from nitrogen fertilisers in China. Across the road from the hotel were some expensive jewellery and electronics shops: at least in Beijing, consumerism was well established. The conference field trip took us out into the countryside to see some experimental rice paddies. The crop is one of the few for which special silicon fertilisers are used to improve yields, and hence the conference. Rice is the most important cereal in China and it is vital to maintain or improve production to feed the country's massive population. To avoid the traffic, I got an early taxi to the airport for my return flight. We passed hundreds of high-rise blocks, and I noticed that each apartment had its own air conditioning unit. I wondered how much energy all of these units would be using, and how much coal was being burnt to power them. It was interesting to get a small snapshot of Beijing, a very rapidly developing city that well illustrates the connected issues of increases in human population and human consumption.

A global perspective on human population

World population reached seven billion late in 2011, and on 7 August 2020 we were already at 7.8 billion, well on the way to eight billion.[3] Yet this very rapid growth is a relatively new phenomenon: it took the whole of human history to reach one billion in 1800, but population has approximately doubled since 1970. The reasons for this population explosion are complex, but they include lowered infant mortality, increased longevity and better sanitation and health care. A massive 36.2 per cent of the world's population live in just two countries, China and India.

The good news is that population growth is slowing in many countries. By 2017, the high-income countries of the world and those of central and eastern Europe, central, south-east and east Asia, and Oceania had a fertility rate of less than 2.1 children per woman.[4] This is regarded as the minimum rate needed for the replacement of the population, and so these areas will see declines in population unless there is significant migration into them from elsewhere. According to Stein Vollset and his colleagues, global human population is now expected to peak at 9.73 billion in 2064 and then decline to 8.79 billion by 2100. These estimates of population sizes change as scientists obtain more data.

It seems there are two key variables that affect the population sizes obtained with these models. The first is how quickly fertility will decline in sub-Saharan Africa. The keys to this are education and the availability of contraceptives. The Sustainable Development Goals (SDGs) have target 3.7 of SDG3, 'Good health and well-being', which states, 'By 2030, ensure universal access to sexual and reproductive healthcare services, including for family planning, information and education, and the integration of reproductive health into national strategies and programmes.'[5] If this target were met, it is estimated that the global population in 2100 would not be 8.79 billion, but 6.29 billion. The figures for sub-Saharan Africa alone are very telling. In 2017 the area had a population of 1,026 million people, and this is predicted to rise to 3,071 million by 2100. But if the SDG target was met then the figure is predicted to be just 1,585 million at 2100. So improved education and access to contraception are huge variables determining the future of population growth in Africa.

The second key factor in controlling future population size is what will happen to countries when fertility rate falls below 2.1? In some countries the fertility rate is already well below the replacement value. Will reproduction rates increase again, and if so when, or will the population continue to decline? These rich countries are worried that their birth rates are too low and that this will cause social instability, with a large ageing population being supported by a small working population. Some countries have already been giving incentives in an effort to increase reproduction. So Sweden has seen an increase in its fertility rate from 1.5 in the late 1990s to 1.9 in 2019. However, these efforts have failed elsewhere, and in 2017 the fertility rate was only 1.26 in Singapore and 1.04 in Taiwan.

Just a brief look at human population trends shows how complex the whole topic is and how difficult it is to make predictions into the future. It is clear, though, that population will increase rapidly from 7.8 billion now to a predicted peak of 9.73 billion in 2064. That is nearly two billion more people on an already crowded planet. There are some that try to divorce human population from its environmental impact, but we are not of the opinion that this can be justified.

Moreover, there are two other problems that are inextricably linked with human population: poverty and consumption. We say more about the battle against poverty in chapter 9, but it is obvious that poor people will consume much less of the world's resources than rich people. Although we have made positive strides in the battle against poverty, in 2015 it was still estimated that 65 per cent of the world's population lived in poverty (defined as living on less than $10 a day) and 10 per cent are in extreme poverty (less than $1.90 a day).[6] Many of these people live in sub-Saharan Africa, families which have an average of between four and seven children.

A global perspective on consumption

Consumption is usually defined in one of two ways: 'consumption of material resources or the consumption of goods and services (also known as economic consumption) that are the direct inputs to human well-being'.[7] Not all consumption refers to material resources. However, humans are consuming both renewable materials (e.g. water, wood and food) and non-renewable materials (e.g. energy and minerals), and chapters in this book are devoted to water, energy and food.

Consumption patterns vary around the world, with rich countries consuming more, and many poor countries unable to do so because of economic restraints. In our globalised society, production of material resources often happens at a considerable distance from where the resources are eventually consumed, so we have concepts like 'embodied water' and 'embodied energy', where those resources may effectively be exported elsewhere. Developed world countries sometimes appear to show some reductions in carbon emissions when production and emissions have been exported to emerging or developing countries. As economic development happens, consumption tends to increase, and we have certainly seen this in the cases of China and India.

For the poorest people in the world, the main drivers of consumption are being able to obtain tolerable living standards, basic commodities and services. These aims were laid out in the SDGs, and we will return to the topic in chapter 9. As countries develop, though, the drivers change. At an individual level, habits can be important. For instance, India has always been a country with a largely vegetarian diet and that habit is persisting even as the country rapidly develops. This is not the case in China, where there has been a shift to a more meat-based diet as the country has developed.

Competitive consumption can be an important driver, where people feel caught in a rat race or have to 'keep up with the Joneses'. In developed countries, the struggle to attain higher income will frequently drive consumption. People feel happier when the economy is expanding and their income is increasing, and are much less happy when the economy is shrinking, which we call recession. At a national level, governments are often fixated on Gross Domestic Product (GDP) as a measure of economic growth, but GDP has now also become a driver of consumption. Governments encourage their workers to produce more in competition with other countries so that GDP will increase. During periods of recession, governments suggest that people should shop rather than save. The age structure of a population can also affect consumption patterns. Older people spend more than younger people on utilities, services and health care, and much less on clothing, motor vehicles and education.

A simple equation

In the 1970s this simple equation was developed during a debate on resource use and population growth: $I = P \times A \times T$ (where I = Human impact on the environment, P = Population, A = Affluence and T = Technology). The equation does have some truth to it, but it is an oversimplification. Let us take the example of climate change. Obviously, the bigger the human population, the more people there are to carry out activities leading to carbon emissions. The amount of emissions per person depends very much on their affluence, so, at the moment, people in the developed world emit a lot more than those in the developing world. However, nations such as Spain that are switching very rapidly to renewable energy sources (see chapter 6) are using technology (T) to *decrease* their impact on the environment.

Looking at table 2, we can see how increased population had affected Beijing when I visited in 2011. As the Beijing environment is highly urbanised, impacts on some factors, such as biodiversity and water, were not immediately obvious during my visit, but many other impacts were. Human population growth and consumption affect almost all of the issues discussed in the other chapters of this book.

Table 2 Interactions of human population and consumption with other environmental issues

Chapter	Beijing story	Global population effects	Global consumption effects
2 Biodiversity	Beijing's growth led to destruction of habitats	Destruction of natural habitats	Biodiversity loss
		Change in land use	Overfishing
3 Climate change	Smog; workshop on greenhouse gas emissions	Increased number of carbon emitters	Increased consumption in developed and emerging nations leads to increased carbon emissions
4 Water		More drinkers and users of water resource	Competition for scarce water resources
5 Human population	Population growth 1400–2011		More consumers
Consumption	Jewellery and electrical goods; cars	More consumers	
6 Energy	Increased car use Air conditioning	More people who need to consume energy	Decreased supplies of fossil fuels
7 Soil		More demands on soil resource	Soil degradation through forest clearance for agriculture
8 Food	Rice production causing nitrogen pollution	More people needing food	Possible over-consumption and a switch to a diet with more meat
9 Environment and sustainable development		Increased population in developing world	Justice: overuse of resources in developed world

So what is needed? On population (P), the biggest need is for decreased growth in the developing world.

This can only happen as people are enabled to move out of poverty and will come through education. Where there is affluence (A), we need to find ways of cutting consumption. Again, this partly requires education: we need to persuade people that they can live satisfying lives without so much 'stuff'. However, it should be noted that if world resources were shared in a sustainable way, everyone would need to have lifestyles similar to those in Mali.[8] In their 2012 report, the Royal Society concluded that we needed to give attention to both population growth and consumption:

> The sustainable development debate has, over recent years, been typified by those who argue that population growth is the source of current unsustainable trends, and those who believe that consumption is the primary culprit. This artificial distinction is unhelpful as it can lead to argument over whether policy should focus on reducing population growth or on improving the sustainability of consumption, while both are clearly important.[9]

We can only reach a more just world, where there is greater parity of standards of living, if we reduce the rate of population growth alongside increasing the living standards of the poorest people.

Finally, what about technology (T)? Technology can help us seriously decrease our impact on the environment, but it should not be seen as a 'silver bullet'. It will not solve all of our problems, and it would be highly unwise to put all of our faith in it. There are many proposed techno-fixes for climate change, but we are uncertain, as yet, if any will work. If we keep doing good scientific research, maybe some solutions to our problems will be found, but, until they are found, it is essential that we work on decreasing our population and our consumption.

A question from the back of the room

On the 'Hope for Planet Earth' climate change tours, almost every night the same question came from the audience, and it still comes up over ten years later. It is phrased something like this: 'But you have not considered the elephant in the room. It is all very well talking about climate change, but the real problem behind it is human population growth.' If you are not prepared for it, it can floor an unwary speaker. After all, you have come to give a talk on climate change. Suddenly shifting on to a totally different, and potentially hazardous, topic can be rather worrying. Having read the first part of this chapter you should already have some parts of a reasonable answer, but Mark Maslin gives a little extra guidance.[10]

First, not all people have contributed equally to the climate change problem. So far, the United States and the European Union have each contributed about a third of the historical carbon emissions, while Africa has only contributed 3 per cent. The richest 10 per cent of people on the planet contribute half of the emissions, and the poorest 50 per cent of people only add 10 per cent of the emissions. So it is the heavy consumers of the rich countries that are the big problem, not the poor countries, even with their rapidly expanding populations.

Second, one might argue that when these poor people get richer, they will add to the carbon-emissions problem. But by the time they do manage to move out of poverty, we would hope that the world will have changed to a low carbon economy (see chapter 6); if we have not, we will be in big trouble.

So, although there is some link between the size of human population and climate change (more humans equals more emissions), it is not a simple one. Still, Maslin points out that, 'While it might not be an immediate solution to the climate emergency, stabilising the world's population is still important.' The effects of our larger population go beyond just climate change. There are many other impacts, some of which are shown in table 2.

Biblical reflection: God's sovereignty and human responsibility

Who takes responsibility? Lessons from the 2008 financial crash

The 2008 financial crash had a major and long-lasting impact on the world. It will be remembered worldwide as one of the scariest moments of financial history for large institutions, smaller businesses and individuals, as people held tight, wondering if their savings, businesses or mortgages would weather the storm. What caused it? There were multiple causes: low inflation and stable growth fostered risk-taking, and the central banks and regulators failed to prevent unwise lending, one example being pooled sub-prime mortgages. The booming Asian economies and the Euro led to risky international investing and borrowing. A further cause was food prices, which rose dramatically between 2005 and 2008 because of complex factors including fuel price increases, biofuels using agricultural land, export restrictions and poor weather consistent with climate change.[11] In the end, according to an analysis in *The Economist*, 'the whole system was revealed to have been built on flimsy foundations; banks had allowed their balance sheets to bloat but set aside too little capital to absorb losses'.[12] What lessons can we learn from this episode for our use of the Earth's resources? The themes of 'risk taking' and borrowing without foundation have parallels in the way we are using up our environmental capital. Forests and other natural resources are being used well beyond their ability to replenish. This usage is being driven by consumer demand; high human populations also have an impact, especially as the emerging economies begin to catch up with the traditionally wealthier west. In a similar way to the sub-prime mortgages, there can be a tendency to sidestep responsibility for negative environmental impacts from commercial activity, but the massive negative impacts on the Earth are all beginning to add up. At some stage, there will be a tipping point, and there could be an ecological crash that will have a similar domino effect to the global financial crash. The difference is that, whereas finances are recoverable, if the ecology of the planet really crashes, it would not be quickly reparable. In the 2020s we are dominated by climate change and the impact of the Covid-19 pandemic. We have seen that the pandemic had its origins in the environmental crisis, and its impacts are vastly greater than the impact of the 2008 financial crash.[13] How should Christians respond to these challenges?

A tension within Christian understanding

One of the recurring tensions in Christian thought is between the sovereignty of God and human responsibility. Those Christians who believe that everything is predestined by God have tended to focus on worship, study, fellowship and holiness of life. Those who lean more towards the view that God expects people to make choices have had a stronger sense of personal responsibility for issues in the world and have tended to be more outward-looking and activist. Clearly this is a generalisation: very many in the former group are socially engaged, while very many in the latter are highly committed to worship and holiness, and there are 'shades of grey' between the two. But it is helpful to understand these trends, in order to make an informed Christian response to both population and consumption.

Understanding creation and the sovereignty of God

Two very different passages linking creation and the sovereignty of God are the 'whirlwind discourse' in Job 38 to 42 and Ephesians 1:3–14. As we discussed in chapter 2, in the book of Job, God puts creation centre stage and seems to impress on Job that he is simply a part of this wonderful interconnected universe.[14] The sovereignty of God is very evident. He laid the Earth's foundation and made the clouds it's garment; he provides food for the raven and has the eagle soar to his command. In the face of this speech, Job replies, 'I know that you can do all things; no purpose of yours can be thwarted' (Job 42:2). We could respond to this passage by deciding that we cannot affect the health of the planet and our own population, because it is in God's hands, but we would also need to acknowledge that God has an infinite care for the rest of his world, as well as humanity.

When we move to Ephesians 1, we find a different starting point. Humans begin centre stage and are blessed and chosen to be holy. The writer is speaking specifically about followers of Christ, who he declares are 'predestined... for adoption to sonship though Jesus Christ' (v. 5). This adoption is by God's grace and is the result of redemption through the cross (v. 7). We might feel that the writer sees creation simply as a backdrop for the salvation of humanity, but from there the lens zooms out and we see the bigger picture: 'He made known to us the mystery of his will according to his good pleasure, which he purposed in Christ, to be put into effect when the times reach their fulfilment – to bring unity to all things in heaven and on earth under Christ' (vv. 9–10). Human salvation is God's plan, but he has a wider purpose, which is to unite all things under Christ.

In both these passages, the sovereignty of God is demonstrated: in Job the emphasis is on his sovereignty over creation and in Ephesians the focus is first on those chosen and then on the ultimate unity of all things in heaven and on Earth. These passages might still leave us feeling that it is for God to bring everything together, while our role is to be faithful to him as he does it. Is there more to the story?

Creation, Christ and human responsibility

A third passage will help us understand the role of Christians more specifically. In Colossians 1:15–20, we see that Christ is chief (first-born) over creation and also head of the church, which is his body. Christ holds creation, and the logical conclusion is that the church, as his body, takes a part in that holding.[15] This takes the tension between God's sovereignty and human responsibility into a different dimension. God is moving creation towards an ultimate fulfilment but he does not expect humanity to take a passive role. If the church is called to share the 'holding of creation', we need to embrace that responsibility as active partners with God. This means that we are called to worship and to holy living, but we also have a gospel imperative to demonstrate holiness in relation to our active engagement with the world. We cannot simply sit back and leave the future of the environment in God's hands, because he has given it to us as our responsibility.

When I (Margot) was 17, my dad started me off learning to drive. I had a few proper lessons but mostly learned from him. He was a great teacher! I was in the driving seat but he was alongside. I could have taken control but I was wise enough to follow his instructions (especially when he said 'Stop!'). As I grew more skilled, my driving became a partnership. As we hold creation with Christ, we have responsibility, while we can also trust in God's sovereignty.

Population: sovereignty and responsibility

In the light of God's sovereignty, how do we respond to the difficult question of our rapidly rising human population? Reducing population growth simply comes down to having smaller families. This is a difficult issue to tackle as it touches on the most important part of many people's lives. In the west, the birth rate is low, yet each person has a carbon footprint many times that of those who live in poorer countries where the birth rate is much higher. The Roman Catholic Church is known for its concern about artificial birth control, and there are Protestant groupings who oppose the limitation of family size.[16] Part of their reasoning is that sex should be procreative and that it is God's will for us to have larger families, based on passages such as the command to 'be fruitful and increase in number' (Genesis 1:28) and the story of Onan, who was condemned for 'spilling his seed' (see Genesis 38:9–10). Some Christians see contraception as unnatural and therefore against God's commandments. However, this must be set against other medical advances that have 'unnaturally' diminished infant mortality and lengthened life expectancy.[17] A careful examination of Onan reveals that his real crime was deception.[18] Another argument against contraception derives from the belief that, because humans are made in God's image (Genesis 1:26), we should not limit population. We need to see these passages in the light of Job 38 to 42, Ephesians 1 and Colossians 1, and of God's love and care for his whole creation.

In chapter 3 we explored covenant and the concept that Jeremiah's prophecy about the 'law written on our hearts' would have originally been a message to the Jewish exiles, who needed to take scripture written for one situation (independence in the land of Israel) and apply it when they found themselves somewhere very different (in exile in Babylon). Today, our situation with regard to population size is on a totally different scale, compared with nations in biblical times. The law on our hearts must surely point us towards honouring God by seeking a level of human population that can live sustainably with the rest of creation, without being condemned to poverty. Achieving that level will require a shift in thinking for many religious and secular groupings worldwide. There also needs to be substantial support. Reduction in family size usually follows an increase in development of a country. The difficulty is that the development itself is often hugely damaging to the environment, which in turn has a knock-on effect on the poorest people. As the environment deteriorates, hope of escaping poverty recedes into the distance. As well as supporting communities in sustainable development, we need to work out ethical ways to support family planning that can enable increased stability and sustainability.

Family planning in Uganda

Christian Connections for International Health (CCIH) provides a forum for Christians working in reproductive health in East Africa. They are promoting family planning from a faith perspective and have been very successful. In Uganda, nearly half of all health care is delivered by faith organisations, and the majority of these provide family planning support. CCIH seeks to equip faith leaders with information and training to enable them to provide a biblical basis for family planning. Community volunteers are trained and provided with bicycles to enable them to reach their communities. Methods include natural family planning, and the initiative has been successful with Protestant, Catholic and Muslim communities.[19]

The emphasis is on helping couples space the timing of their pregnancies. When births are close together, the second child is more likely to be undernourished and therefore vulnerable. Edith Irongo and her husband Charles (archdeacon of the Kyando in Busoga Diocese, Uganda) used family planning to space their four children. This enabled them to support each child properly and pay for their education. They use their family as an example when they give marriage preparation and Edith discusses it at Mothers' Union meetings. Archdeacon Charles believes that spiritual matters and practical matters, like the healthy timing of pregnancies, are connected: 'The church provides family planning because we think about spiritual health and the health of the body. They both are important to take care of the whole person.'[20]

Consumption: sovereignty and responsibility

As we have seen, consumption is the flip side of population. There are plenty of biblical principles that encourage us to live more simply. The Old Testament includes instructions on tithing and gleaning (Leviticus 19:9–10; Numbers 18:21), which illustrate the principle of generosity towards those who have less. Jesus, too, encouraged simplicity of life (see Matthew 6:25–34). Our trip to Spain included a wonderful retreat with Christian theologian and songwriter John Bell. He spoke of consumerism as something that binds us, so that we need to be released from it. Christian discipleship in the 21st century involves a reassessment of our values. If we don't reassess, future generations will pay the price for our overconsumption.

The good news is that living more simply can mean living in a more satisfied way. For example, Adam Martin and colleagues found that people were more positive and alert when they switched from driving to walking or cycling to work.[21] Those who are wealthier, in rich and poor countries, have a huge responsibility and very real choices to make as we seek to restore the planet to the healthy life-giving state that pleases God.

Rebuilding a kinder and more sustainable world

When lockdown happened in spring 2020, shopping became more and less complicated – more complicated because of all the restrictions, and less complicated because we all simply made do. We used up flour and other dried and tinned items in the cupboards that had been hanging around for a long time; we didn't think of buying clothes, because a change of a pair of jeans, a few T-shirts and a couple of 'Zoom shirts' (to look nice in front of the laptop) seemed to do the trick. Though we were not major buyers of fashion or other items, we had been consumers. It was good to stop and think.

For several years, A Rocha UK ran a programme called 'Living lightly'. It was led by Ruth Valerio and encouraged people to live in a way that made a lighter footprint on the planet and was more connected with their local communities. Ruth is now director of global advocacy and influencing at Tearfund. In the Grove Booklet we wrote on Covid-19, Ruth reflected on the changes in society during lockdown.[22] Communities became more connected as people helped and supported each other. As the virus spread around the world, we realised that we are interconnected with one another and with the environment. We realised that people are more important than the bottom line of the economy, and we started valuing key workers and people in low-paid jobs that are essential to our lives. There was also a realisation that changes could be made quickly when needed and we have an opportunity to rebuild our economy in a better way.

Our vision is to see rebuilding based on the foundation of these values. We need to prioritise local communities and ways of living lightly to give the planet space to renew itself. This means finding ways to build an economy that is not based around endless consumerism and waste. Our electrical goods have become essentially disposable. If one part breaks down, there is no means of repair. There seems no choice but to throw away and buy new. Can we change our economy to make things repairable? Many communities are now running repair cafes that help people repair basic items from chairs to coffee makers. How can we use these ideas to build back better? Our world is highly interconnected but continues injustices from the past, with millions of people living in poverty. How can we rebuild a fairer global economy that will eradicate poverty and help to stabilise human population without increasing consumerism? These are huge questions but essential ones to engage with as we work out our Christian discipleship in the 2020s.

Major shocks to civilizations in the past have resulted in a shift to a different way of organising societies and economies. Aspects of the culture that were already under strain, collapse and something different takes over. Through the pandemic we have had a harsh light shone on many aspects of our world that are unjust and unsustainable. Our task is to use our gifts to be part of building a better world and one that points more clearly towards God's future peaceable kingdom.

God's delight and our covenant call

God's sovereignty, seen in Job and Ephesians 1, concludes with God's delight in his creation and his care of it. Our responsibility is seen in Colossians 1:15–20. It is bound up with our own life in Christ and shows his redemptive care for our world. As we seek to live lightly on God's Earth, so we will find ourselves working within the sovereign purposes of our God, who loves all he has made.

ECO TIP Your church could be a collecting station for non-doorstep recycling, for items such as mobile phones, batteries, printer cartridges and reading glasses. In doing this, you will show your care for the Earth and a commitment to using its resources wisely. In the summer you could have a place where people could leave surplus vegetables for those who don't grow them. You could run a repair café for your community. All these ideas need volunteers!

Bible study: making life-giving choices

Read 1 Peter 4:1–11

You may like to start by discussing the drivers of consumption in rich and poor countries. Are we trapped into any of them? Peter wrote this letter to Christians who were trying to make sense of suffering and work out how to live in a world that was hostile to their faith and values.

1 How do we make choices to live according to the will of God, and what might they involve (vv. 1–2)?
2 Each generation faces new challenges. In what ways does our consumption today mirror the evils of Peter's time (v. 3)? Are we as effective in resisting it (v. 4)?
3 In what ways (if any) will a simpler and more self-controlled lifestyle help us to pray (v. 7)?
4 How do we show the love and generosity of the gospel in a world with global poverty (vv. 8–11)?
5 How can we glorify God better when approaching the issues of population and consumption (v. 11)?

Notes

1 'Demographics of China', *Wikipedia*, **en.wikipedia.org/wiki/ Demographics_of_China** (accessed 7 August 2020).

2 J. Nye, 'China starts televising the sunrise on giant TV screens because Beijing is so clouded in smog', *Mail Online*, 17 January 2014, **dailymail.co.uk/news/article-2540955/Beijing-clouded-smog-way-sunrise-watch-giant-commercial-screens-Tiananmen-Square.html** (accessed 7 August 2020).

3 Worldometers, 'Current world population', **worldometers.info/ world-population** (accessed 7 August 2020).

4 S.E. Vollset et al., 'Fertility, mortality, migration, and population scenarios for 195 countries and territories from 2017 to 2100: a forecasting analysis for the Global Burden of Disease Study', *The Lancet*, 14 July 2020, **doi.org/10.1016/S0140-6736(20)30677-2**.

5 United Nations, 'Good health and well-being (SDG 3)', **un.org/ sustainabledevelopment/health** (accessed 7 September 2020).

6 M. Roser and E. Ortiz-Ospina, 'Global extreme poverty', **ourworldindata.org/extreme-poverty** (accessed 10 August 2020).

7 The Royal Society, *People and the Planet*, The Royal Society Science Policy Centre report 01/12 (2012).

8 J.P. McKeown, 'Population and ecological sustainability', in C. Bell and R. White (eds), *Creation Care and the Gospel* (Hendrickson, 2015), pp. 175–91.

9 The Royal Society, *People and the Planet*, p. 60.

10 M. Maslin, 'Stabilising the global population is not a solution to the climate emergency – but we should do it anyway,' *The Conversation*, 7 November 2019, **theconversation.com/stabilising-the-global-population-is-not-a-solution-to-the-climate-emergency-but-we-should-do-it-anyway-126446** (accessed 10 August 2020).

11 D.D. Headey and S. Fan, 'Reflections on the global food crisis', *IFPRI Research Monograph*, 2010, **ifpri.org/publication/reflections-global-food-crisis** (accessed 7 August 2020).

12 'The origins of the financial crisis: crash course', *The Economist*, 7 September 2013, **economist.com/schools-brief/2013/09/07/crash-course** (accessed 1 September 2020).

13 R. Valerio et al., *Covid-19*.

14 H.H. Shugart, *Foundations of the Earth: Global ecological change and the book of Job* (Columbia University Press, 2014).

15   M.J. Hodson and M.R. Hodson, *Climate Change, Faith and Rural Communities* (The Agriculture and Theology Project, 2011).

16   J.P. McKeown, 'Receptions of Israelite nation-building: modern Protestant natalism and Martin Luther', *Dialog* 49 (2010), pp. 133–40.

17   J.M. Sleeth, '6.5 billion and counting: A Christian case for small families', *Christianity Today*, March/April, 2007, **booksandculture. com/articles/2007/marapr/8.36.html** (accessed 4 September 2020).

18   McKeown, 'Population and ecological sustainability'.

19   K. Erb, 'Religious leaders as family planning advocates in Uganda', *Christian Connections for International Health*, 2014, **ccih.org/ religious-leaders-family-planning-advocates-uganda** (accessed 12 August 2020).

20   K. Erb, 'Religious leaders provide health as well as "food for the soul"', *Christian Connections for International Health*, 2019, **ccih. org/religious-leaders-provide-health-as-well-as-food-for-the-soul** (accessed 12 August 2020).

21   A. Martin, Y. Goryakina and M. Suhrcke, 'Does active commuting improve psychological wellbeing? Longitudinal evidence from eighteen waves of the British Household Panel Survey', *Preventive Medicine* 69 (2014), pp. 296–303.

22   R. Valerio et al., *Covid-19*.

 ENERGY

Renewable energy in Spain

Travelling through Spain on our sabbatical trip in 2014, one thing that became very obvious was the number of wind turbines there. In parts of the countryside they were on every hilltop. They did not seem out of place; after all, Spain is the country of Don Quixote, who famously 'tilted at windmills'. Certainly we saw no signs of protests against wind turbines in Spain, although they are not allowed in National Parks or close to habitations. The whole renewable energy story is changing rapidly, so where does Spain stand in 2020?

The provinces of Burgos in the north and Albacete in the south-east are currently the biggest producers of wind energy.[1] Spain's wind energy capacity is impressive, and in 2020 it is fifth in the world behind China, the United States, Germany and India, with 4 per cent of the total world installations.[2] Wind met 20.8 per cent of national electricity demands by 2019, and the country has 1,203 wind farms.[3] Like all technologies, though, wind turbines are not without their problems. On our journey around Spain, we twice saw large flocks (numbering 20 to 40) of Griffon vultures, a very impressive sight. Sadly, the vultures are common victims of collision with wind turbines, as a study of the birds in southern Spain showed.[4] Most of the mor-

talities happened when the birds were migrating in October and November, and switching off the turbines at times when the birds were spotted in the area reduced mortality by 50 per cent, with only a 0.07 per cent decrease in energy production. Poorly sited wind turbines

cause many more bird deaths than those that are well sited, but deaths from this source have to be put in context.[5] We like cats, but our furry friends kill far more birds than do turbine blades.

Spain also has a very well developed solar industry, with southern Spain having some of the best sunshine in Europe. There were some regulatory problems that decreased the growth of solar power in the country, and, from 2008, the strong recession in Spain led the government to cut its subsidies to the industry. Despite these problems, Spain remains (in 2018) eleventh in the world for total solar energy production.[6] As we saw in chapter 4, Spain has many hydroelectric facilities, and there is also a small amount of biomass burning for energy. Renewable energy provided 37.4 per cent of Spain's needs in 2015, of which 19.1 came from wind power, 11.1 from hydroelectric, 5.1 from solar and 2.0 from thermal. An environmental policy introduced by Spain in 2018 will see the country aim to obtain 75 per cent of its electricity from renewables by 2030, and 100 per cent by 2050. This will involve a massive deployment of renewable technologies.

A global perspective on energy

If you ever watched an old film about the oil industry, you might remember the 'gushers'. The oil rig drilled into the deposit and oil spurted out of the well head under its own pressure. The problem then was controlling it. That oil was easy and cheap to get at, and it was a rich source of energy. Things have changed since then, and oil is now much more difficult and costly to extract.

Here we will introduce the concept of 'Energy returned on energy invested' (EROEI).[7] To get the oil out of the ground involves an investment of energy beforehand, including constructing the rig and drilling the hole, and transport costs. If we can calculate the amount of energy used to obtain the oil and we know how much energy is derived from burning it, then we can determine the EROEI. It is the same for all forms of energy (see table 3). Back in the 1920s, oil had an EROEI of

100:1, but the figure has fallen considerably to about 20:1 as we have exploited all of the easy oil.

Table 3   Energy returned on energy invested (EROEI) for various energy sources (extracted from Zencey, 2013 with updates* from Rana et al., 2020[8])

Energy type	Average	High estimate	Low estimate
Oil	19:1		5:1
Coal		85:1	50:1
Natural gas	10:1		
Hydroelectric		267:1	11:1
Nuclear		15:1	1.1:1
Wind inshore*		58:1	34:1
Wind offshore*		17.7:1	16.7:1
Solar photovoltaic*		34:1	5:1
Rapeseed biodiesel*		2.6:1	1.1:1
Tar sands oil	5:1		
Wave	15:1		
Tidal	6:1		

The energy sources listed in table 3 all have some disadvantages, but it is clear from chapter 3 that we need to move away from fossil fuels because of the dangers of climate change, and we need to do so as soon as possible. We can only keep going with fossil fuels if technologies like carbon capture and storage (CCS) prove to be effective. Here, the carbon dioxide from the burning of fossil fuels is captured and stored underground. CCS has been proven to work in relatively small-scale projects, but whether it can be developed on a large scale, in time to affect climate change scenarios this century, is doubtful. Nuclear energy took a major hit in the aftermath of the Fukushima disaster in Japan in March 2011. Concerns over safety and long-term storage of waste remain. So, if we rule out fossil fuels and nuclear energy, we are left with renewables (wind, solar, hydroelectric, wave, tidal, biomass and biofuel). Certainly, apart from coal, renewables match up fairly well with other sources in terms of EROEI. Coal is hugely polluting, both in terms of carbon dioxide and other pollutants, such as sulphur dioxide and soot. In many parts of the world coal is being phased out as gas and renewable energy is cheaper. But the big question is could we power our society simply on renewables?

In 2013, Zencey considered that we would need our main fuels to provide something like 5:1 EROEI to keep an industrial civilisation like ours going. He thought that the main problem is what is called the 'energy trap'. To build the infrastructure for a major shift to renewables, we need to use energy, and at the moment much of our energy is provided by fossil fuels. Just in terms of EROEI, it makes more sense to stick with oil, as the infrastructure for that has already been built. A more recent analysis of the problems of the transition from fossil fuels to renewables was provided by Iñigo Capellán-Pérez and his colleagues in 2019.[9] They modelled a rapid transition to a 100 per cent renewable electric system globally by 2060. This suggested that there would be a decrease in the EROEI of the energy system from a current value of about 12:1 to about 3:1 by 2050, stabilising later at about 5:1. These values are well below those needed for industrial societies. Often it seems that political and economic barriers are the principal problems in making a transition to renewable energy, but the EROEI of the system also needs to be considered. Moreover, this study revealed that to make the energy transition may lead to critical shortages in the availability of some metals, particularly those needed for solar energy. The authors emphasised the importance of recycling these materials. Clearly managing the transition to a world powered by renewable technologies is not without its problems.

The other problem with powering our civilisation just using renewables is that they may take up a lot of space and completely change the appearance of the countryside. The late David MacKay looked into this possibility for the UK and concluded, 'To sustain Britain's lifestyle on renewables alone would be very difficult. A renewable-based energy solution will necessarily be large and intrusive.'[10] We may be faced with a choice between wind turbines and solar panels or runaway climate change.

Climate change, stranded assets and divestment

We had long been aware of climate change, but it was at a conference in Oxford in 2002 that we fully realised the seriousness of the situation. The conference was put on by JRI in the UK and the Au Sable Institute in the United States, and we were representing A Rocha.[11] It had a big effect on efforts to make the church in the States take the issue more seriously, but it also marked a major watershed for us, eventually leading us to take part in the Hope for Planet Earth tours (see chapter 3). Martin has since racked up hundreds of talks and lectures on climate change.

The topics of climate change and energy use are intimately linked. It seems that a decrease in the availability of 'easy' conventional oil has meant that energy sources that were uneconomic a few years ago have been explored or exploited: deep sea oil, Arctic oil, tar sands and fracking. Many of them have harmful effects on the environment besides climate change. The big question now is whether we can use all of these unconventional sources, or indeed, the remaining conventional sources. In 2012, top NASA climate scientist James Hansen said that it would be 'game over for the climate' if the Alberta tar sands were ever to be exploited.[12] The battle over this is still continuing. After considerable pressure, then President Barack Obama eventually ruled out building the Keystone XL pipeline, which would pipe the tar sands down to Texas for processing. However, his successor, Donald Trump, rapidly reversed this decision, and this has led to a further battle in the courts and on the ground. With the election of Joe Biden in November 2020, it looks likely that the pipeline may face even more difficulties.[13]

If we are to avoid dangerous climate change, Bill McKibben has suggested that we need to leave a large amount of fossil fuel reserves in the ground.[14] In January 2015, a major report was published in the journal *Nature*, suggesting that 82 per cent of global coal reserves, 49 per cent of gas and 33 per cent of oil will need to remain unburnt if we are to have a reasonable chance of keeping under the 2°C safety limit that most scientist think is advisable.[15] Even larger amounts will be required to remain under ground if we wish to aim at the 1.5°C target suggested by the Paris Agreement. That will require rapidly phasing out the burning of these fuels. Not surprisingly, the fossil fuel industry has, for many years, not been at all keen on this idea. They have lobbied very hard against legislation that might reduce the use of fossil fuels and spent huge amounts of money on funding climate scepticism.[16] The worry for the fossil fuel industry is that if governments decide to cut carbon emissions (as they should), and renewable energy sources continue to grow, then fossil fuel reserves may seem a poor investment and become uneconomic. These are known as 'stranded assets', reserves that the fossil fuel companies have marked up for use but which cannot be burnt.

The resistance from the fossil fuel lobby led McKibben and his organisation, 350.org, to start a campaign to persuade organisations to divest from fossil fuel investments.[17] The idea first gained a lot of interest in the United States, where universities, churches and communities have divested. The movement then spread worldwide, with the World Council of Churches divesting in 2014. In the UK, the Quakers, the British Medical Association, Oxford City Council and the Universities of Bristol and Glasgow are just some of the high-profile organisations to have divested. The reasons for divestment vary, but it is often done on moral, ethical or health grounds. On the eve of the Climate Summit in New York in September 2014, the Rockefeller Brothers Fund and a coalition of philanthropists pledged to divest from more than $50 billion (£31 billion) in fossil fuel assets. In 2015, the Church of England decided to divest from tar sands and thermal coal but was also attempting to engage with fossil fuel companies to influence their strategies on climate change.[18] At their July 2018

General Synod meeting, they decided that they would divest from all fossil fuel investments in those companies not unequivocally aligned with the Paris Agreement by 2023.[19]

Fracking

We tend to be environmental pragmatists, and don't always come up with the deep green answer. So in the last ten years or so we have spent quite some time considering the pros and cons of fracking, also known as hydraulic fracturing. In fracking a well is drilled and fluid is injected at high pressure into the ground. This fractures the shale rocks and releases gas, which is then used as an energy source.

Arguments in favour of fracking tend to centre on energy security, lower gas prices and a good environmental footprint compared with other fossil fuels.[20] It is also frequently touted as a 'bridge to renewables', giving us the time and energy to build the necessary infrastructure for renewables. However, there are a number of problems with this technology that have been widely reported: earthquakes (mostly of a minor nature); contamination of groundwater; leakage of methane from wells; and the burning of gas, which contributes to climate change. The first three can be reduced if best practice is adopted. The EROEI of fracking is not that easy to determine, but Moeller and Murphy estimated this at 10:1, taking all stages of the process into account.[21] According to their analysis this is close to the value obtained from solar photovoltaic. They also pointed out that fracking wells have steep decline rates in production, meaning that new wells continually needed to be drilled. Moreover, drilling has so far concentrated on the best areas for shale gas, and production will further decline as more marginal areas are used.

So, overall, there are some advantages to fracking and most of the difficulties can be overcome with good management. But the problem that it still involves burning fossil fuels is a big one. We cannot see how committing to this technology and building an infrastructure for it is a good idea when we need rapid decarbonisation. Fracking has advanced very rapidly in the US, but has undoubtedly had more problems in the UK. In November 2019, the UK government halted fracking, after earthquakes above safety limits were reported at the only active fracking site at Preston New Road in Lancashire.[22] The future of fracking in the UK is now in doubt.

Transport

Not long after we moved to Haddenham in 2009 we bought a new car. Well, new for us, but two years old. We did lots of research trying to find the perfect green car. Although there are only two of us, we needed something fairly big as we often transport boxes of books and display stands to speaking engagements. In the end we went for a Citroen Picasso, diesel automatic. It has been a great car for us, very economical, and we took it all around Spain and Portugal for our 2014 sabbatical. But slowly our 'perfect green car' became less perfect, and now we recognise that although it is pretty good on carbon emissions, as a diesel it is not great for nitrogen oxide and particulates.

At least we have not been living in cities, and so our pollution has been dispersed. In addition we have always only had the one car between us, and use trains and buses a lot. But when we moved from Haddenham to Filkins in summer 2019, getting a new car was rising to the top of the list. We run our cars as long as we can, and we know it is getting near time to change. When we do change we want an electric car, but we need one with a reasonable range. We were just about to move on this when the pandemic hit, and our mileage dropped considerably. There was no point in buying a new car if we were not going anywhere! 2021, maybe...

We have given quite a lot of thought about transport in the last few years, and Martin was involved in organising what we think was the first ever Christian conference specifically on the topic in 2018. There are many resources from this meeting on the JRI website.[23] The issues with transport are hugely complex. Reducing carbon emissions from our travel is one of the hardest parts of getting to net zero emissions. It is also one of the more difficult environmental problems we face at a personal level, and we will look at that in the next section.

Measuring our carbon footprint

Caroline Pomeroy has been director of Climate Stewards,[24] one of the A Rocha family of organisations, since 2013. She gave a seminar at the JRI transport conference in 2018. Here she tells us how we can measure our own carbon footprint, most particularly from transport:

> I well remember the shocked expression on the face of a man who takes frequent business trips to China when building his carbon footprint out of Duplo[25] on the Climate Stewards stand at the 2019 Greenbelt Christian festival. He could see clearly how a return flight emitted about the same amount (three tonnes) of CO_2 as his whole year's car mileage.
>
> Understanding our carbon footprint is a very helpful first step in comparing the climate impact of different activities and establishing a baseline from which we can measure improvements. The average person in the UK has a carbon footprint of around eight to ten tonnes, excluding international flights. If embodied emissions (emissions from the production of goods overseas but bought in the UK) are included, this rises to around 14 tonnes or more!
>
> Measuring carbon footprints is a complex task, requiring reliable data on the carbon emissions from each input; decisions about where to draw the boundaries of what we are measuring; and clarity on what assumptions we are making. Climate Stewards' online carbon calculator[26] enables individuals to calculate the carbon footprint from their flights, land travel, energy used in the home and food. While carbon emissions from burning oil, gas, etc. are relatively easy to measure, others are more complicated. For transport, we take 'emissions factors'

(i.e. kg of CO_2 emissions per passenger mile) and multiply them by the distance travelled. The emissions factors for flights include a 90 per cent increase to cover radiative forcing (the fact that emissions high up in the atmosphere have a greater environmental impact than ground-level emissions). Carbon emissions associated with food are calculated using 'proxy' data which gives a carbon emissions figure based on how much things cost. 360°Carbon[27] is another online tool which enables churches and other organisations to measure their carbon footprint. It covers the same areas as the personal footprint calculator, as well as other expenditure on building and office costs.

Caroline will return in chapter 9 to tell us about the other end of Climate Stewards' work in Africa and elsewhere. Climate Stewards is realistic that, though we must cease using fossil fuels as rapidly as possible, this needs to be managed as we change world economies and our own lifestyles. How are the energy providers responding? Steve Hughes was CEO and later chair of the trustees for A Rocha UK, but he had previously worked in the oil industry. We asked him about his career and his thoughts on sustainability and oil companies.

From oil to A Rocha

For 32 years I worked for a major oil company in a range of senior human resources roles. Some 15 years ago I felt that the time had come to move on and, after a year's theology course at the London School of Theology, I joined the Christian environmental charity A Rocha UK as their chief executive. For me this was a logical move in terms of my long-term support of A Rocha's aims and my concern for the natural world. However, it was not out of disillusionment with my employer. While there were some policies within the oil company with which I would have taken issue, the major objective of finding, producing and refining oil was one which they sought to fulfil ethically, safely and in an environmentally friendly way, as part of their licence to operate. We need oil companies to operate in an acceptable way as long as we consume oil products.

They were very different-sized organisations, but for me the challenges of working in the oil company and of working in A Rocha were very similar. They were about people, about budgets and about business principles, and so the personal transition was very straightforward. My former colleagues were a little bemused at my switch, but supportive as they knew where my passions lay (I had chaired the company's Christian fellowship and had taken many of them birdwatching!). My new colleagues among the environmental community were accepting of me despite my history.

There is a risk in the ongoing debate about divestment that the oil companies are simply demonised, which does not do them justice. What they do needs to be done and, while we should hold them to account for how they do it, it is going to remain their core business. The majority of the technologies of renewables do not fit well with their expertise and cost base. So my plea from both sides of the fence would be for dialogue and understanding. We do need to reduce our dependence on fossil fuels, but we do need them produced.

The future of energy

Things change very rapidly with the energy topic. The Covid-19 pandemic of 2020 changed things again. For a time global oil prices dropped through the floor as the use of transport ground to a halt in the lockdowns around the world. Then, fairly rapidly people started talking about 'building back better'.[28] Having seen some benefits for the environment caused by the lockdowns (cleaner air, quieter roads, hearing birdsong), there was some determination not to return to 'business as usual'. A key factor in building back better is undoubtedly moving away from fossil fuels and switching to renewable technologies as quickly as possible.

Professor Piers Forster, working with his teenage daughter, Harriet, and a team of experts looked at both the short-term effects of lockdown and the longer-term impacts of green recovery programmes.[29] They found that the carbon emissions cuts during lockdown will have a negligible effect on global warming. However, if we see economic recovery programmes that favour a green stimulus and reductions in fossil fuel investments, then we could still stay within the target of 1.5°C above the pre-industrial temperature suggested by the Paris Agreement.

In August 2020, the oil company BP announced that it was intending to cut its fossil fuel production by 40 per cent by 2030 and that it would move into renewable and bioenergy technologies.[30] This seems at odds with what Steve Hughes said above. However, at the same time as the BP announcement, it was reported that Greenpeace had discovered that the company had been using a fund that was specifically set up for the transition to low carbon technologies for work within the fossil fuel sector.[31] Mel Evans of Greenpeace said that BP had carried out a 'masterclass in greenwashing'. Moreover, Tony Juniper, now chair of Natural England, responded to the BP announcement on Twitter:

> In 1997 @bp_plc rebranded as a clean energy company with the slogan 'Beyond Petroleum'. Then shareholders ordered management 'back to petroleum' so as to increase short term profit. In the process they destroyed value and created what is now a stranded asset.[32]

In other words, BP had followed this route before, but had then gone back on it. We hope BP will be able to make the change and it would certainly be in their shareholders' interest, but there is considerable scepticism from a whole variety of sources about whether the fossil fuel companies will change course. As we write, in summer 2020, it is too early to tell whether 'building back better' or 'business as usual' will prevail.

Biblical reflection: Sabbath and sustainability

Sundays on our Spanish trip felt a little nostalgic, with a reminder of how things used to be back in Britain. There were not a vast number of people going to church, but all the shops were closed and the towns and villages had a definite 'sabbathness' about them. A stray dog or cat might be wandering around, and from a bar or restaurant you could hear the sounds of people relaxing. Only the foreign tourists were out, hard at it with guidebooks and walking poles in hand. I was reminded of these sabbath days in April 2020 when lockdown caused a sense of perpetual Sunday in our Cotswold village. We took walks along the local lanes and found others out walking or breezing past on bikes. Farmers were active but the main road was still. The world was impossibly busy for many key workers and very difficult for others, but as the world shut down there was a sabbath moment to reflect. The 24/7 nature of many countries and cities simply reflects our relentless approach to the world's resources, including ourselves. Ultimately, sabbath means putting a brake on our use of energy. It is a call to turn the switch off for a while.

Sabbath and release from work

Sabbath is the last part of the creation narrative. After the explosion of energy to create the universe, God takes a day to rest (Genesis 2:2). In Jewish tradition, sabbath is part of creation and makes it complete.[33] It is interesting that the day described as 'holy' was the one day when divine energy was stilled and no creating was done. This is an important message for our energy-intensive world. There is sanctity about setting activity aside: it is the most holy aspect of creation.

Walter Brueggemann describes sabbath as a release from the endless restlessness that typifies a production-driven society.[34] Taking the Exodus story, he casts Pharaoh as a restless personality driving a repressive culture that demanded unending production (Exodus 1:11–14). The request for a break for the Israelite slaves was met with higher demands: the Israelites had to collect their own straw for making bricks (Exodus 5:1–21). Brueggemann points out that they were building store cities for Pharaoh, where he could accumulate ever more grain and wealth. The economy had become a caricature of the providence storehouses of Joseph, who built up supplies of grain against a predicted drought (Genesis 41:41–57). Joseph sold the stored grain and Pharaoh found that the surplus food had the potential to generate wealth. Abundant food from a booming economy also enabled population growth, and the growing Israelite population became a threat to Pharaoh. So he put them to forced labour to continue to build the economy. The store cities that had been a blessing became a form of oppression, but the exodus from Egypt gave salvation from this oppressive regime.

Life in the wilderness needed significant change and adjustment, and this proved difficult. The people needed to transition from an urban and agricultural society built on surplus wealth to being nomadic herdspeople again. For many this would seem a backward step, as it required them to live in tune with the natural environment around them. They needed to trust God rather than the abundant food that the repressive life in Egypt did at least provide (Exodus 16). Manna could be collected only for each day, apart from the eve of the sabbath when a double portion could be gathered. Some Israelites were unable to make the shift and continued to store up and to seek to gather on the sabbath. The adjustment took time and was fully realised only through a change of worldview that came from the covenant at Sinai. Meeting God in the desert and on the mountain brought Israel into a relationship with him once again.

As we look at the development of energy in our society, we can see how the discovery of fossil fuels revolutionised our potential to develop prosperity. However, our dependence on them has now become oppressive and dangerous. We need to reduce energy use and change to more renewable energy sources. These changes may look like a backward step to many people. Few in my parents' generation rode a bike after they had bought a car. Yet I am fitter because I ride a bike. How can society shift? Entering into a worldview of sabbath is a way forward for our culture.

Sabbath at the heart of a new society

Because we are made in God's image we share his capacity to take a sabbath rest. We share his ability to stand back, reflect and have joy at being still. We share his capacity to love our neighbour and to share God's gift of rest both with our human neighbours and with animals and the rest of creation (Exodus 20:8–11). When we deny this rest to others, we do not deny their image of God but we deny our own and diminish ourselves. We devalue the Earth that is God's creation.

The concept of sabbath was expanded in the Old Testament to include a sabbath year every seven years and a Jubilee year every 50 years (Leviticus 25). In these years the land was to lie fallow and everyone was to be given a rest, including servants and animals. People would need to live on accumulated food from previous years and from what the land produced spontaneously. Other laws developed this idea of building slack into the system. Farmers were not to harvest to the very edges of their fields and were to leave the gleanings (missed grain) for the poor to collect (Leviticus 19:9). A whole way of life was set up that was very different from the economic culture in Egypt, where profits were maximised by every possible means. A Jewish scholar, Michael Fishbane, describes entering sabbath as a process of 'divestment'.[35] On entering we find a sphere of inaction that releases us from the pressures of our normal working lives. We find ourselves able to appreciate creation as a gift. It is a process that leads to thankfulness.

Community sustainability groups

Around the UK and across the world, there are many local community groups that are dedicated to sustainability. Some also have an emphasis on food growing, cycling or wildlife. All of them have a commitment to support healthy natural environments, reduce energy use and support communities' living in greater harmony with the natural world. There are various networks and these often overlap. You may find one in your local area bearing the prefix 'sustainable', 'low-carbon' or 'transition'. If there is not one already, you can find a few friends and start one!

During our time in Haddenham we were involved in a sustainability group that formed as a transition group and is now called Zero-Carbon Haddenham. Transition is a movement of communities coming together to reimagine and rebuild our world. It aims to help communities respond to the challenge of climate change and the need to move to a post-carbon economy. It does this by nurturing caring and entrepreneurial communities that develop skills and initiatives for the benefit of all.[36] As we shared in chapter 3, we joined the newly formed Haddenham in Transition soon after we arrived there, and together we started to think of ways in which we could encourage energy reduction in our community. Haddenham in Transition pioneered several direct energy-saving projects in the village, including thermal imaging of people's houses and air-tightness testing, enabling people to find the draughts in their homes. These initiatives helped people see where they were losing heat and how to make their houses more energy efficient. There were community projects to encourage people to develop local food and 'be more local'. These included a community apple press and an annual 'Homemade in Haddenham' day in the village hall. We held community picnics on the village green and had films and talks to raise environmental awareness, including a film shown in St Mary's Church, powered by cyclists! Transition members helped establish other initiatives in the village, including Townsend Community Orchard and Haddenham Syrian Family Project (that enabled a refugee family to come to this country by providing a home and support in the community).

Before we left Haddenham in 2019, we held a goodbye bring-and-share meal at the vicarage for all those involved in Haddenham in Transition over the ten years we were there. In our last few years in village, the group had become less active, mainly because every-one had become involved in other related work (one became the first Green Party district councillor in Buckinghamshire). Martin put together a PowerPoint loop featuring the projects we had developed over the years. When everyone saw how much we had achieved together they started saying that Transition must get going again. So as we left Haddenham the group restarted, under the new name of Zero-Carbon Haddenham, with a monthly repair café run jointly with St Mary's, Caféplus+, and a new tree-planting project called reLEAF.[37]

The older community organisations in the village have come to respect Zero-Carbon Haddenham as a key partner in community cohesion. There has been collaboration across traditional divides. For exam-ple, our Green Party councillor joined forces with our Conservative councillor to try to save a village pub. In seeking energy reduction and valuing all things local, it is helping the village community to develop an inbuilt sense of rest and recreation. Local produce and businesses, local activities and friendship networks are all valued. It points us towards a world where there is space to breathe.

Sabbath and renewal

The three themes of creation, covenant and rest undergird the concept of sabbath. In the early Church, Sunday was seen not simply as the first day of the week but as the eighth day.[38] In celebrating the resurrection of Jesus there is a sense of entering into a space that is beyond time. Sabbath points back to creation, is lived in the present and points forward to the reality of the new creation. When we stand back and look at our present society, built on fossil fuel energy, it is clear that we are in a short and very unusual phase in history. Fossil fuels have given some cultures riches beyond our wildest dreams, but at a terrible cost. As we look at the alternatives, it is certain that we need to have a plan to move away from fossil fuels for ourselves, our communities, our nations and the global economy. The principles of sabbath provide good news: life would be better if we could make that transition well.

There are many websites where you can find good advice on saving energy. A good one is run by the Energy Saving Trust.[39] There are simple suggestions, such as switching things off when you are not using them, then more advanced ideas, such as loft insulation and installing solar panels for heating water and generating electricity. With the help of our friends in Transition, we found where our vicarage was losing most heat. We put a long curtain over the front door and we blocked the chimney when not in use. We have now moved to a much older vicarage, which is a bigger challenge, but the down-to-earth solutions of thick curtains, more loft insulation and simply shutting internal doors are all helping. We've discovered that you can still be warm in a cooler house by wearing warmer indoor clothes. If you are not already using a renewable-energy supplier, you might like to make this switch and you may find your bills are cheaper. For churches there is a scheme called the Big Church Switch.[40]

Bible study: sabbath, new wine and fresh approaches

Read Luke 5:33–39

John's disciples are concerned that Jesus' disciples are not serious enough about their faith. Jesus' disciples are new believers and he explains that they need new and flexible approaches. He describes himself as a bridegroom who rejoices with his bride.

1 What can we learn from Jesus' approach to his disciples to help our own approach to new or younger Christians (vv. 33–35)?
2 We don't patch clothes unless we value them and want to continue using them. How can we adapt our homes, our churches and other aspects of our lives to downsize our energy use?

3 We need new approaches to energy use but these will require us to think about how we live our lives in new ways. How can our faith help us to take this step (vv. 36–38)?

4 People tend to want to stick with what they know. How can we present the 'new wine' in a way that will draw others to want to try it? (v. 39)

Read Luke 6:1–10

This passage is about Jesus and the sabbath. It again shows the need for more flexible, life-giving approaches.

5 How can we take the three principles of creation, covenant and rest to help our church be more life-giving to every member?

6 How can we make time to be part of our wider community and help it develop in a positive way?

Notes

1 F.G. Montoya, M.J. Aguilera and F. Manzano-Agugliaro, 'Renewable energy production in Spain: a review', *Renewable and Sustainable Energy Reviews* 33 (2014), pp. 509–31.

2 Global Wind Energy Council (GWEC), *Global Wind Report 2019*, 25 March 2020.

3 Spanish Wind Energy Association (AEE), **aeeolica.org/en** (accessed 13 August 2020).

4 M. de Lucas, M. Ferrer, M.J. Bechard and A.R. Muñoz, 'Griffon vulture mortality at wind farms in southern Spain: distribution of fatalities and active mitigation measures', *Biological Conservation* 147 (2012), pp. 184–89.

5 R. Webster and F. Roberts, 'Bird death and wind turbines: a look at the evidence', *CarbonBrief*, 10 April 2013, **carbonbrief.org/ bird-death-and-wind-turbines-a-look-at-the-evidence** (accessed 13 August 2020).

6 'Installed solar energy capacity, 2018. Cumulative installed solar capacity, measured in gigawatts (GW)', **ourworldindata.org/ grapher/installed-solar-pv-capacity** (accessed 13 August 2020).

7 E. Zencey, 'Energy as master resource', in Worldwatch Institute (ed.), *State of the World 2013: Is sustainability still possible?*, Kindle edition (Island Press, 2013), ch. 7.

8 R.L. Rana, M. Lombardi, P. Giungato, and C. Tricase, 'Trends in scientific literature on energy return ratio of renewable energy sources for supporting policymakers', *Administrative Sciences* 10, no. 21 (2020), **doi.org/10.3390/admsci10020021**.

9 I. Capellán-Péreza, C. de Castroa and L.J.M. González, 'Dynamic energy return on energy investment (EROI) and material requirements in scenarios of global transition to renewable energies', *Energy Strategy Reviews* 26, no. 100399 (2019), **doi.org/10.1016/j. esr.2019.100399**.

10 D.J.C. MacKay, *Sustainable Energy: Without the hot air* (UIT, 2009).

11 Hodson and Hodson, *Cherishing the Earth*, pp. 193–196.

12 J. Hansen, 'Game over for the climate', *The New York Times*, 9 May 2012, **nytimes.com/2012/05/10/opinion/game-over-for-the-climate.html** (accessed 14 August 2020).

13 F. Spotted Eagle and K Mackey, 'Biden must be our "climate president". He can start by ending pipeline projects', *The Guardian*, 23 December 2020, **theguardian.com/commentisfree/2020/dec/23/**

biden-must-be-our-climate-president-he-can-start-by-ending-pipeline-projects (accessed 8 January 2021).

14   K. Bagley, 'The most influential climate science paper today remains unknown to most people', *Inside Climate News*, 14 February 2013, insideclimatenews.org/news/20140213/climate-change-science-carbon-budget-nature-global-warming-2-degrees-bill-mckibben-fossil-fuels-keystone-xl-oil (accessed 14 August 2020).

15   D. Carrington, 'Much of world's fossil fuel reserve must stay buried to prevent climate change, study says', *The Guardian*, 7 January 2015, theguardian.com/environment/2015/jan/07/much-worlds-fossil-fuel-reserve-must-stay-buried-prevent-climate-change-study-says (accessed 15 August 2020).

16   M.J. Hodson and M.R. Hodson, *The Ethics of Climatic Scepticism* (Grove Booklets, 2015).

17   Fossil Free, gofossilfree.org (accessed 27 September 2020).

18   A. Vaughan, 'Church of England ends investments in heavily polluting fossil fuels', *The Guardian*, 30 April 2015, theguardian.com/environment/2015/apr/30/church-of-england-ends-investments-in-heavily-polluting-fossil-fuels (accessed 15 August 2020).

19   Operation Noah, 'Church of England General Synod votes for fossil fuel divestment', 8 July 2018, operationnoah.org/news-events/church-of-england-votes-for-fossil-fuel-divestment (accessed 15 August 2020).

20   B.K. Sovacool, 'Cornucopia or curse? Reviewing the costs and benefits of shale gas hydraulic fracturing (fracking)', *Renewable and Sustainable Energy Reviews* 37 (2014), pp. 249–64.

21   D. Moeller and D. Murphy, 'Net energy analysis of gas production from the Marcellus shale', *Biophysical Economics and Resource Quality* 1, no. 5 (2016), doi.org/10.1007/s41247-016-0006-8.

22   J. Ambrose, 'Fracking halted in England in major government U-turn', *The Guardian*, 2 November 2019, theguardian.com/environment/2019/nov/02/fracking-banned-in-uk-as-government-makes-major-u-turn (accessed 15 August 2020).

23   'Transport now and in the future – what are the issues?' JRI Conference, March 2018, jri.org.uk/events-2/transport-now-and-in-the-future-what-are-the-issues (accessed 15 August 2020).

24   Climate Stewards, climatestewards.org (accessed 15 August 2020)

25   'Duplo footprint', climatestewards.org/resources/duplo-footprint (accessed 15 August 2020).

26   'Carbon footprint calculator', **climatestewards.org/offset** (accessed 15 August 2020).

27   360° Carbon, **360carbon.org** (accessed 15 August 2020).

28   OECD, 'Building back better: a sustainable, resilient recovery after Covid-19', *OECD Policy Responses to Coronavirus (Covid-19)*, 5 June 2020, **oecd.org/coronavirus/policy-responses/building-back-better-a-sustainable-resilient-recovery-after-covid-19-52b869f5** (accessed 17 August 2020).

29   P.M. Forster et al., 'Current and future global climate impacts resulting from Covid-19.' *Nature Climate Change*, 2020, **doi.org/10.1038/s41558-020-0883-0**.

30   S. Nasralla and R. Bousso, 'BP to cut fossil fuels output by 40% by 2030', *Reuters*, 4 August 2020, **reuters.com/article/us-bp-outlook-idUSKCN2500NH** (accessed 17 August 2020).

31   M. Cuff, 'BP using fund meant for low-carbon technology to invest in fossil fuels', *inews.co.uk*, 3 August 2020, **inews.co.uk/news/bp-fund-low-carbon-technology-invest-fossil-fuels-569923** (accessed 17 August 2020).

32   Tony Juniper tweet, 10:14 am, 5 August 2020.

33   J. Sacks, *Faith in the Future* (DLT, 1995), p. 134.

34   W. Brueggemann, *Sabbath as Resistance* (John Knox Press, 2014).

35   M. Fishbane, *Sacred Attunement: A Jewish theology* (University of Chicago Press, 2008), quoted in Brueggemann, *Sabbath as Resistance*.

36   For more information about Transition, see **transitionnetwork.org** (accessed 15 August 2020).

37   For more information about Zero-Carbon Haddenham see **zeroch.org** (accessed 21 September 2020).

38   M.R. Hodson, *A Feast of Seasons* (Monarch, 2000), p. 182.

39   Energy Saving Trust, 'Energy at home', **energysavingtrust.org.uk/energy-at-home** (accessed 9 January 2021).

40   The Big Church Switch, **bigchurchswitch.org.uk** (accessed 9 January 2021).

 SOIL

A steep learning curve

In September 1989, I (Martin) arrived at Oxford Polytechnic (now Oxford Brookes University) for my first full-time lecturing job in plant physiology. The first module I had to teach was 'Soils and plant growth', a topic of which I had fairly limited knowledge. My degree in botany had involved a few lectures on soils, but that was over ten years before, so I had to get up to speed very rapidly on a whole body of knowledge before the students arrived in October. I remember visiting Warren Farm, near Horton-cum-Studley, north of Oxford, where we took the students to look at soils in the field and collect samples for analysis back in the lab. Working on the samples also involved a whole lot of soil chemistry, which was not bad for me as chemistry had always come fairly easily. It seems obvious, but we also needed to look at water in soils. Nutrient uptake by plants was fairly familiar, but fertiliser chemistry was new to me. Somehow I kept ahead of the students and made it to Christmas!

I ran 'Soils and plant growth' for many years, and hundreds of students passed through it. I was always pleased when they discovered just how interesting (and important) soils are. Many started on the module thinking it was just another module but left with a different view. Teaching soils expanded my horizons (the soil scientists among you will groan at this point!), and it influenced my research work. Even now, my recent work on carbon sequestration requires a good knowledge of soil biology and chemistry.

A year after my arrival in Oxford, my department, in collaboration with the Department of Planning, launched a new master's degree in environmental assessment and management. This course was aimed at producing people who would work in environmental impact assessment (EIA). This was a rapidly advancing area at the time, and building developments over a certain size needed to conduct an EIA as part of the approval process. So if you were building an airport, an oil refinery or a road, you needed an EIA. The EIA looked at ecology, noise, pollution, social impact, visual impact, archaeological impact, geology, soils and just about everything that a development might affect in an area. The assessors then recommended ways of mitigating the impact of the development. In some cases the EIA might throw up something that suggested the development was not a good idea. Naturally I ended up teaching the impacts on soils. There was some information available, but it was in widely dispersed sources, and I needed to bring it all together to make a coherent story.

The Master's proved very popular and our course team was asked to write a book on the subject matter contained in it. I wrote the soils chapter. The book came out in 1995, and it obviously met a need, going into four editions. For the second, third and fourth editions I was joined by four soils consultants as co-authors: Roy Emberton, Kevin Hawkins, Hugh Masters-Williams and Chris Stapleton (see below for Chris's life story). Their real-life experience complemented my academic approach, and I like to think that by the fourth edition we had laid a firm foundation for future work on soils and EIA.[1] It was exciting to be in on the development of a new sub-discipline from the beginning.

So I have a special affection for soils, and am pleased we have a chapter here in which to focus on a topic that is often missed out of environmental discussions.

What is soil?

Most people think of soil as the dirty, brown stuff in which you grow plants in your garden. Wikipedia puts it like this: 'Soil is the mixture of minerals, organic matter, gases, liquids and a myriad of organisms that can support plant life.'[2] That is not a bad definition. There are two main types of soil: organic and mineral. Organic soils develop in wet places and consist mostly of organic matter. Peat is a good example. In most parts of the world they are not that common, but where they do occur they are often important for nature conservation (for example, in fens), and they are highly significant carbon stores, keeping carbon out of the atmosphere.

Most soils are mineral soils with a substantial mineral content that is usually derived from the bedrock. The size of the mineral particles in the soil determines its texture. So sandy soils have large particles, but with a relatively small surface area. Clay soils have small particles with a huge surface area which gives these soils their water-holding properties. They have very different properties; compare digging sand on a beach with digging a clay soil in a garden. The organic content is mostly derived from decaying plant matter (leaves, for example). In mineral soils this is quite a small component, but it has a major role in helping to stick the soil together. When soils lose their organic matter they are much more susceptible to erosion.

Two soil components, water and oxygen, are often overlooked, but the balance between them is hugely important. Most plants need a good supply of water, but also require oxygen for root respiration. Too much water results in waterlogged soil, which restricts oxygen supply and badly affects most plants, even causing them to die (rice is an obvious exception). Too little water means a drought, which, if it goes on for a while, will also kill the plants.

One of my earliest scientific memories is some homework I was set at primary school. Accompanied by my mother, wielding a torch, we investigated our front lawn one autumn evening. As the teacher expected, we observed earthworms dragging recently fallen leaves into their holes. Earthworms and other soil organisms are involved in the continual recycling of materials within the soil. I am not sure whether on that autumn evening I quite anticipated how much of my lifetime I would spend looking at soils!

A global perspective on soils

We rely on soils for growing most of our plants, and for most of our food. Our farm animals eat plants before providing us with milk, eggs and meat. Some greenhouse crops are now grown hydroponically (in water culture, without soil), but we would be in serious trouble without soil. Unfortunately, for a number of reasons, we are losing soil at a fairly alarming rate. Some of the big problems for soils are erosion, compaction, salinity, pollution and urbanisation. Let us look briefly at each.

By far the biggest problem globally is soil erosion. This is caused by two factors: water and wind. Water erosion happens when raindrops impact the soil and cause soil particles to be ejected, and when water runs across the soil's surface detaching soil material and washing it into watercourses. Water erosion is worst in areas with high rainfall, and where vegetation has been removed, exposing the soil, in places with moderate rainfall. Wind erosion only happens when the soil is dry and the particles do not stick together. Flat, open landscapes are where wind erosion is the greatest issue, and so, in the UK, East Anglia is worst affected. Some of the figures for erosion rates are very worrying. Each year about ten million hectares of cropland are being lost, and in many areas we are losing soil at a rate that is 10–40 times faster than the rate at which the soil can naturally regenerate.[3] Loss of vegetation cover is a major accelerating factor in erosion, which is why deforestation is so devastating, particularly in high rainfall tropical areas. Most recently, David Wuepper and his colleagues showed major differences between countries in their rates of soil erosion.[4] Sometimes these differences were even visible between neighbouring countries from aerial photographs of the border between two countries, and the factor that seemed most responsible for the difference was dependence on agriculture.

Compaction is usually caused by vehicles driving over the soil. This decreases the spaces between the soil particles, meaning roots cannot penetrate as easily, and water cannot sink as easily into the soil. This is why water is often seen lying in vehicle tracks on a farm or building site after rain. Ploughing soil can alleviate surface compaction, but may not reach compaction at depth. Then so-called traffic pans may develop, restricting water movement and root growth to the upper layers of the soil.

My first ever scientific paper appeared in 1981 in the *Arboricultural Journal*. It concerned the dumping of salt piles, intended to aid in road de-icing, under mature trees.[5] The idea was to shelter the salt from rainfall, but it leached into the soil and was taken up by the tree, causing damage or even death. We looked at a mature beech tree in mid-Wales, and found that the salt was transported up the side of the tree facing the salt dump. It did not directly kill the tree, but honey fungus attacked the weakened tree and eventually killed it some 25 years later. My co-author and I launched a small campaign to inform local authorities about the problem. Nowadays most roadside salt is stored in plastic bins, so maybe our campaign had some effect! The bigger worldwide problem with salinity, however, concerns arid-zone agriculture, particularly when land is irrigated. Even slightly salty irrigation water is a problem. Imagine a pot of boiling salty water on a stove. The water evaporates, but the salt becomes concentrated in the remaining liquid. The same happens in arid areas when they are irrigated, and the salt accumulates in the upper layers of the soil. Most crops have their growth reduced or are killed by saline soil. So every year large areas of agricultural land go out of production because the soil has become too salty.

There are many ways that soil can become polluted. In some cases the pollution is relatively localised. My interest in metal toxicity in plants has led me to visit a number of metal smelting sites in my career. I did my undergraduate and postgraduate work in Swansea in the mid to late 1970s at a time when the Lower Swansea Valley Project was very active.[6] The area had been badly affected by contamination left behind when metal smelters were abandoned, and the project was engaged in a major clean-up operation in the valley. I was very involved with the local conservation volunteers during my time in Swansea, and we planted hundreds of trees to help restore the environment. I have returned to Swansea many times since, and a considerable transformation has been achieved. In our previous book we told the story of Sudbury in Ontario, Canada, where the metal contamination was far worse than in Swansea.[7] A major example of long-distance soil pollution is acid rain, which is produced when sulphur dioxide from power stations reacts with water in the atmosphere. This can travel hundreds of miles from the source of the pollution to the destination.[8]

At the moment our towns and cities take up about 1 per cent of the land surface area of the world, but that figure is growing rapidly. As the population increases (see chapter 5) so more housing is needed, and more land is built upon. Settlements are often sited in areas of good agricultural land, and, once it is urbanised, land is effectively lost for ever to agriculture. If we lose our agricultural land then food security might be threatened. Like many settlements in the southern UK, Haddenham saw a massive increase in building on agricultural land in the ten years we were there. I (Martin) once made a comment about potential food-security problems in the future on one of the big planning applications, but I never had a response. In a small, heavily populated country like the UK we have to balance building projects against protecting our best agricultural soils for the future. That is where the soils component of EIA mentioned above comes in.

My life in soils

Chris Stapleton knows a lot about soils and EIA. I got to know Chris around 30 years ago, and we co-taught soils on the master's degree course at Oxford Brookes until 2017. We also co-authored the soils chapter in the last three editions of *Methods of Environmental and Social Impact Assessment*.[9] This is Chris' story:

Leave school as I did with an odd mixture of A-levels (geography, chemistry and English literature) and your choice of degree in those days was limited to geography. Going for a practical application of this subject I ended up graduating from Reading University in 1975 with a degree in soil science.

Joining the Ministry of Agriculture, I found myself working in the planning system, carrying out soil surveys in areas under pressure from urban development. The aim of the surveys was (and still is) to try to protect our best quality land and to restore mineral sites back to agriculture, forestry and wildlife habitats. Thrown in at the deep end, I had to give evidence at public inquiries, defending the results of my surveys and being cross-examined by stern QCs, who were determined to undermine my evidence on behalf of their developer clients. It was a character-forming experience.

I extended the scope of my environmental work to manage teams of other environmental specialists (including ecologists, landscape architects, hydrologists and others) carrying out EIAs of large development projects. Here the objective is to minimise the impact of development on the wider environment, not just on soils and agriculture. As a nation the UK has been protecting its best-quality land from the late 1960s onwards, and now restores surface mineral sites to good standards. In more recent years it has to be said that the level of protection of agricultural land has been relaxed to some extent, but this has been balanced by a greater emphasis on protecting soils to maintain a wider range of functions as an important part of wildlife habitats and part of the hydrological cycle.

This is all very worthy, but it gives no sense of the deep satis-faction that comes from having used my expertise in soils for over 40 years. It has given me a job with the freedom, mostly as a self-employed consultant, to travel all over England mainly (but also Scotland and Wales), and to walk all over the countryside as the seasons change. I have learned to read the landscape (its combination of geology, landforms, hydrology and soils), and this insight into how the natural environment works is some-thing that few others will experience. I continued to carry out my soil surveys until my late 50s and my final role was to work on the impacts of the proposed HS2 railway on agriculture and soils. I retired in 2018 and looking back on my career, I think that field survey work beats an office job.

The soils of Spain

On our sabbatical trip around Spain we were very aware that Spain is an agricultural nation. In chapter 4 we saw something of just how important water is in Spain, and how this resource is managed. What about the soil? Not surprisingly erosion is a major factor, and it has been going on for a long time.[10] There is evidence of erosion from the Bronze Age and also from Roman times. During the Medieval period erosion increased, leading to sedimentation and the infilling of estu-aries such as at the mouths of the Andarax River (south-east Spain), the Vélez River (Málaga, Andalucía), and the Turia and Júcar Rivers (eastern Spain).

More recently, in the 20th century (particularly since the 1960s), thou-sands of hectares of farmland in the mountains have been abandoned as the rural population has moved to the cities. This has led to the spread of vegetation on the mountains and decreased erosion. At the same time there has been some expansion of almond and olive orchards and vineyards on to marginal lands, often on steep hill slopes. This has led to increased erosion, especially during heavy rain. During our nine-week trip in 2014 we had plenty of opportunity to sample Spanish wines, and those from the Rioja region were a particular favourite. Unfortunately, vineyards are very susceptible to erosion for the simple reason that the soil in between the plants is usually bare, and exposed to the wind and rain. In the Rioja region, 15–20 per cent of vineyards are on hill slopes with gradients of over 10 degrees, so when it rains, water moves rapidly across the surface of the soil and contributes to excessive erosion.

Carbon sequestration

About 80 per cent of terrestrial carbon is present in the soil, with the rest being in plants and animals. The carbon present in the soil is over three times the amount in the atmosphere, and only the oceans have a larger quantity. As soils have been degraded globally some of that carbon has been lost, particularly through soil erosion. In recent years the topic of carbon sequestration in soils has received increased interest, as it is now recognised that it may have a role in combatting climate change. The big problem is that carbon sequestration in soils is reversible. So the carbon in the leaves that are dragged down into the soil by earthworms each autumn is mostly released back into the atmosphere through respiration within a short time. If we could find ways of slowing that release, it would be a big move forward.

I (Martin) have worked on phytoliths for 40 years. Phytoliths ('plant stones') are formed in plant cells when soluble silica taken up from the soil precipitates out to form a solid mass. The resulting phytoliths take the shape of the cells in which deposition occurs. The solid silica strengthens the plant and is the reason Pampas grass is so sharp, as are the leaves of many other grasses and cereals. Phytoliths are also resistant to breakdown in the soil, and have found many uses in archaeology and palaeoecology. Rather surprisingly, in 2018 I found myself writing a paper on carbon sequestration in phytoliths. Some phytoliths contain substantial amounts of carbon.[11] Could this carbon be trapped there, and be released more slowly? Could this help in the fight against climate change? We don't know yet.

Biblical reflection: Exile and return

When I (Margot) became a rural vicar, one of the things I quickly dis-covered was a strong link between my job and soil. I found myself on local farms, and I had the joy of a garden after life in a city apartment. It seemed that mud always managed to cling to shoes, especially when I was back in the city. Another link with the soil came with my very regular relationship with churchyards. As Haddenham churchyard was nearly full, I worked on a project to encourage and support the village to find a new burial ground, and we hope a major part of it will be for natural burial. This means the land above will be developed as a nature reserve, without physical memorial markers and a digital guide to locate graves.

My contact with the earthiness of life and death has been a reminder of our fundamental connection with the Earth. Genesis 2:7 reminds us that God formed the first human (*adam* in Hebrew) out of the soil (*adamah*) of the Earth. Ancient cultures were keenly aware of their dependence on soil, but in our modern cities it is much easier to forget. We do so at our peril. The theme of exile in the Bible traces the breakdown of people's relationship with the land, as well as with God and each other. As we realise the degree of degradation of our Earth's soil alongside other environmental problems, we can find echoes in the biblical narrative, and the ongoing story of covenant.

Forgetting the covenant

Exile came through a breakdown of the covenant relationships that God gave as a gift to humanity and the Earth. We can trace this through the biblical prophets. In Jeremiah 2:7, the Lord says: 'I brought you into a fertile land to eat its fruit and rich produce. But you came and defiled my land and made my inheritance detestable.' In the context of this passage, the land is 'defiled' because of the immoral and syn-cretistic practices of the people. However, it is clear that powerful people had also taken the gift of land for granted and had abused it. They had not kept the sabbath rests, and this had led to injustice for poorer people under them as well as for animals and the land itself. The Bible makes a strong link between the faithfulness of the people and the health of the land. When the people become faithless (to God, each other and the Earth) then, in biblical thinking, the land suffers. Jeremiah and Hosea say 'the land mourns'. 'There is... no acknowledgement of God in the land. There is only cursing, lying and murder... Because of this the land mourns and all who live in it waste away; the beasts of the field and the birds of the air and the fish of the sea are dying' (Hosea 4:1–2a, 3, NIV 1984). Jeremiah gives a stern warning to the people that, although there is still time to change, unless they turn from their present way of living, the whole land will be ruined (Jeremiah 4).

Many in our own society today might be surprised that the Israelites' actions were having a negative effect on something as basic as soil, let alone the rest of the environment. Yet every time we buy something made of tropical hardwood, or use a product with palm oil in it, we may support an industry that is clearing rainforest, often with devastating effects on the thin soils beneath. In chapter 5, we saw that our consumer lifestyles are driving a massive destruction of our Earth's resources, impacting on every aspect of the environment, including our once stable climate. Scientists and activists have become modern prophets calling for reason and for the world to change from this destructive course of action. Some climate scientists have felt like Galileo, as the policy conclusions based on their work have challenged a powerful establishment struggling to come to terms with the unsustainability of its industries and wealth. In the biblical prophets we see the build-up of tension that leads inevitably towards the exile of the people. As we look at our own culture we see a similar pattern. Will we listen to the prophets in time?

Eventually the people were defeated and taken into exile. Interestingly, the land benefited from this: 'The Land enjoyed its sabbath rests; all the time of its desolation it rested' (2 Chronicles 36:21). The 'exile' for the land had been the earlier period of human apostasy. In the biblical exile period, with a much lower human population, the land was finally able to rest. A bizarre modern example of this is around the failed nuclear power station of Chernobyl in Ukraine. Despite high levels of radiation, the exclusion zone around the plant has created a haven for wildlife, including brown bears, which have been seen for the first time in centuries. A recent study has concluded that birds there are adapting to ionising radiation.[12] This does give hope that the Earth can replenish itself, although it is salutary to realise that humans are a greater direct threat to wildlife than radiation. Our challenge is to enable nature to flourish even in the face of climate change and other problems. We hope it will not be in the absence of humans, a scenario once predicted by James Lovelock in his book *The Revenge of Gaia*.[13] His most recent book proposes that beings born from artificial intelligence will help humans adapt to and mitigate the challenging environmental conditions that lie ahead of us.[14]

Ultimately the message of the exile is one of hope. Israel returned to God, and to a just way of living, and eventually returned to the land. This return is marked by the land's fruitfulness, mirroring the restored relationships. The prophet Zechariah says: 'The seed will grow well, the vine will yield its fruit, the ground will produce its crops, and the heavens will drop their dew. I will give all these things as an inheritance to the remnant of this people' (Zechariah 8:12). This is a managed landscape, indicating that the biblical view of the environment is one where humans have an important role to play in shaping natural systems. Internationally, if different cultures could grasp the need to change and the way to do it, there is a fruitful way ahead. Our approach to the conservation and management of soil is crucial but often overlooked as a priority.

Jesus and soil

The classic example of Jesus talking about soil is the parable of the sower (Matthew 13:2–9). Jesus later gives the interpretation of this parable as the different responses people make to the preaching of the kingdom of God. We can use it to ask an additional question: what did Jesus know about soil and farming? The seed that fell on the path was quickly eaten by birds. The path would have been compacted soil, and Jesus was aware that seed falling on it would not germinate.

Some seed fell on rocky places without much soil. This grew up quickly but withered in the sun. Seed falling on rocky places would not necessarily grow up quickly and Luke does not include that phrase in his version. However, thin soil over a layer of rock will support plant growth after rain, as the water is held near the surface, but it will not allow strong root growth. As the sun dries the soil, the plants will die as their roots have no access to deeper water.

The seed falling among thorns could not compete with these strong weeds and the seedlings were choked, but finally seed fell on good soil and this produced a large crop.

This parable shows considerable knowledge about soil. Jesus would have picked the theme to resonate with his listeners, but it would also have been something that came readily to his thinking. One can only speculate on where Jesus gained this knowledge. It may have come from helping on farms in his youth. It may have been that his family had land, which he had helped to work. The parable conveys an understanding of farming and a respect for the knowledge farmers have of their land and crops.

Partners in Action

Andy Lester is head of conservation for A Rocha UK. Here Andy writes about their Partners in Action scheme:

> The UK Partners in Action network now consists of twelve partners, responsible for caring for 1,049 acres of UK land and all committed to making a big difference for wildlife. Many of these are conference and retreat centres, such as Ashburnham Place

in West Sussex, Hilfield Friary in Dorset and Scargill House in Yorkshire. Others are outward-bound centres like Adventure Plus in Oxfordshire and St Madoc's in Wales. The coronavirus crisis hit the sector hard, and the future for many centres is uncertain. What is clear is that there will be no return anytime soon to 'business as usual'. A Rocha UK will be standing alongside our network to offer prayer support and ongoing practical advice. And the hope is that UK Christian land owners can come out of the crisis with a renewed vision and a determination to realise a future that puts nature conservation at the heart of faith mission.[15]

Soil and faith: Hilfield Friary, Dorset

One of the Partners in Action, and one of Margot's favourite places, is Hilfield in Dorset.[16] An Anglican Franciscan friary, it is also a working farm on the edge of the North Dorset Downs. Going to Hilfield on retreat is like joining a family. Everyone eats together at a common table and worships together in the simple chapel (once a cowshed). There are opportunities to help with the daily life of the community and explore the Dorset countryside. The community manages 50 acres of land and its soil to enhance their environmental value. Here Richard Thornbury, land manager at Hilfield and an A Rocha UK trustee, gives a little background to their work:

> Hilfield has an integrated approach to faith and land management informed by the Franciscan vision of creation. Laid out beautifully in his 'Canticle of the Creatures', Francis shows his deep awareness of creation as a family of brothers and sisters with God the Father, belonging to each other in an unpickable web of interdependence.
>
> Soils, like friaries, are complex communities where every member finds a place and plays its part. There is constant friction and tensions as members rub up against each other, renegotiating their needs and expectations. We all experience

this in our relationships, and yet are compelled to try to make them work because we belong in relationship. In healthy soil communities there is diversity of members: bacteria, archaea, fungi, plants, etc. This diversity is the foundation of resilience and balance grown on the friction between members.

The same is true of the Hilfield community, a mixture of brothers, lay members and guests, young and old, from diverse cultures, with different abilities and expectations. The ideal grasped for is that all are welcomed, included and valued, and tensions and friction are recognised as part of being community.

Underpinning the diversity of Hilfield's ecosystem is a diversity of soil. The friary transverses a cross-section of the North Dorset Escarpment's layers of different soils. On top, the thin chalk supports wildflower meadows. Cattle graze them and are fed hay cut once they've flowered, in turn providing meat for the common table. Next, a layer of greensand. Its light, workable soils were settled early and are still the location of the friary's kitchen gardens. Water is forced to the surface here forming springs, creating wet woodland habitats, one of the most pressured in Europe. These extend on to the clay of the Somerset Levels, the final layer. But it is in the patches and interfaces that the greatest diversity occurs. The pockets of sand over the chalk providing chalk heathland, the landslips with their jumbled geology creating acid fen in a calcareous landscape. Diversity in community is the foundation of resilience and beauty.

ECO TIP If you do not have a garden, you might like to try growing something indoors. You could try some herbs in the spring. Make sure any soil or compost you buy is sustainably sourced. A tip for many seeds is to soak them a little first to help them germinate. If you have a garden why not try to find out the sort of soil you have? When it is moistened, can you roll it into a cylinder with your fingers (high clay) or does it just fall apart (high sand)? You may like to see if you could improve your soil sustainably and increase your yield!

Bible study: soil, figs and vineyards

There are a number of passages about vineyards in the Bible, and the vine is often a symbol of Israel. The following passages differ from the parable of the sower; in these the soil is good but the plants do not produce fruit. The first passage leads up to the prophecies of exile and the second points towards the possibility of salvation and return.

Read Isaiah 5:1–7

1 Share any experiences you may have had with plants not producing the fruit you had hoped.
2 How might God look at our society today? Are we producing good fruit?
3 What might be the consequences of our actions? What would 'exile' be for our culture?

Read Luke 13:6–9

4 Who is Jesus seeking to call back to God?
5 What hope does he offer them?
6 What hope does he offer us?
7 How might we respond to it?

Notes

1 C. Stapleton, H. Masters-Williams and M.J. Hodson, 'Soils, land and geology', in R. Therivel and G. Wood (eds), *Methods of Environmental and Social Impact Assessment*, fourth edn (Routledge, 2018), pp. 63–101.

2 'Soil', *Wikipedia*, **en.wikipedia.org/wiki/Soil** (accessed 4 September 2020).

3 D. Pimentel, 'Soil erosion: a food and environmental threat', *Environment, Development and Sustainability* 8 (2006), pp. 119–37.

4 D. Wuepper, P. Borrelli and R. Finger, 'Countries and the global rate of soil erosion,' *Nature Sustainability* 3 (2020), pp. 51–55, **doi.org/10.1038/s41893-019-0438-4**.

5 L.J. Shaw and M.J. Hodson, 'The effect of salt-dumping on roadside trees', *Arboricultural Journal* 5 (1981), pp. 283–89.

6 S.J. Lavender, *New Land for Old* (Adam Hilger, 1981).

7 Hodson and Hodson, *Cherishing the Earth*, pp. 44–46.

8 Hodson and Hodson, *Cherishing the Earth*, pp. 48–52.

9 Stapleton et al., 'Soils, land and geology'.

10 J.M. García-Ruiz, 'The effects of land uses on soil erosion in Spain: a review', *Catena* 81 (2010), pp. 1–11.

11 M.J. Hodson, 'Can phytoliths save the world?' *JRI Blog*, 2 July 2019, **jri.org.uk/blog/can-phytoliths-save-the-world** (accessed 18 August 2020).

12 I. Galván et al., 'Chronic exposure to low-dose radiation at Chernobyl favours adaptation to oxidative stress in birds', *Functional Ecology* 28 (2014), pp. 1387–403.

13 J. Lovelock, *The Revenge of Gaia* (Penguin, 2007).

14 J. Lovelock, *Novacene: The coming age of hyperintelligence* (Penguin, 2020).

15 'Partners in action', **arocha.org.uk/our-activities/practical-conservation/partners-in-action** (accessed 4 July 2020).

16 Hilfield Friary, **hilfieldfriary.org.uk** (accessed 21 August 2020).

 FOOD

Our mountain hideaway

During our sabbatical trip around Spain in 2014 we stayed five weeks in Pitres, a small village in the Alpujarras region of the Sierra Nevada Mountains. We hired an apartment at La Oveja Verde (The Green Sheep),[1] which was an ideal place for writing. Pitres is not very touristy, and feels as near as one can get to 'real Spain'. It is a great base for walking and we could walk out into the countryside directly from the village. We had a few meals out, but mostly ate in our apartment and bought our food in the village.

Pitres is well served by local shops. There is a small family-run supermarket, which was well stocked. They obviously had a fair number of British visitors as there was a whole shelf devoted to English teabags, digestive biscuits and pickles. The bakery in Pitres sold a few lines of loaves, biscuits and cakes, all freshly baked, and the fishmonger sold quite a variety of fresh fish as the coast was not far away. There is also a butcher, a pharmacist, a doctor, a hairdresser, a stationer, an ironmonger, several bars and a church. Every Friday there is a market in the plaza specialising in fruit, vegetables and clothing. We would always go first to the organic 'Ecologica' stand, run by an elderly farmer whose wife had a sideline in knitting. Our host at La Oveja Verde, José, had a glut of tomatoes, and bags of them would appear outside our apartment door.

On a walk down into the valley below Pitres we heard a horn blaring in one of the smaller villages. A van then came into view, stopped and opened its back door to reveal a mobile fish shop! Soon, local villagers appeared, and were then seen carrying off fish for dinner. The van then moved off to the next village and sounded its horn again. So the smaller villages were well served with fish, and a bread van also did the rounds.

Our five weeks in Pitres were great, and it was interesting to try to work out the food supply system of the village. Maybe its isolation meant Pitres was well served with shops, and local produce seemed the norm rather than the exception.

Food: a global perspective

The world is faced with a major problem with respect to food. In chapter 5 we saw that the global human population is potentially due to rise to about 9.73 billion in 2064, before declining. We have seen that almost whatever we do now, some level of climate change is inevitable (chapter 3), and this needs to be taken into account in any future planning. So how do we feed the world? Here we need to introduce the concept of food security. This was defined at the World Food Summit of 1996 as existing 'when all people, at all times, have physical and economic access to sufficient, safe and nutritious food that meets their dietary needs and food preferences for an active and healthy life'.[2] The good news is that the percentage of people who are undernourished has declined from 15 per cent in 2000–2004 to 8.9 per cent in 2019 despite a 21 per cent increase in world population.[3] Even so, 690 million people still go to sleep hungry each night.

We have managed to feed more people by becoming more efficient. For example, cereal yield increased by 175 per cent between 1960 and 2014, and the amount of land used for cereal production only increased 16 per cent.[4] The difficulty now is that although there is more land that could be brought into production this would have other undesirable effects, including decreased habitat for biodiversity (chapter 2). As we saw in chapter 7 we have also been losing agricultural land to soil erosion, salinisation and urbanisation. It therefore seems likely that more production will be needed from the same amount of land or possibly even less land. We will need to produce an estimated 50 to 100 per cent more food by 2050. But how?

In 2009 the Royal Society suggested that we needed 'sustainable intensification', which they defined as 'the production of more food on a sustainable basis with minimal use of additional land'.[5] They saw genetically modified (GM) crops as key to increased production, but were also supportive of improving conventional agricultural practice and low-input methods. Also in 2009, the International Assessment of Agricultural Knowledge, Science and Technology for Development (IAASTD) released their extensive report.[6] It would be fair to say they had more emphasis on improved practice and less on GM crops: 'Genetically modified plants and GM fish may have a sustainable contribution to make in some environments just as ecological agriculture might be a superior approach to achieving a higher sustainable level of agricultural productivity.'[7] It is now clear that 'sustainable intensification' and IAASTD represent two opposing philosophies, and the battle between their supporters can be intense and even emotional. In 2019, a report by the High-Level Panel of Experts on Food Security and Nutrition (HLPE) of the Committee on World Food Security attempted to survey this whole area, aware that 'it brings together very different and contentious visions for the future of humanity'.[8]

The report laid out six disputed areas, which are briefly summarised as follows:

1 The size of agricultural enterprises: small family farms or large enterprises with economies of scale?
2 The deployment of modern biotechnologies: GM crops or not? (See below.)
3 The deployment of digital technologies: could contribute to improved sustainability, but what is being attempted, by whom and what future is being envisaged?

4   The use of synthetic fertilisers: has led to big gains in productivity, but major problems with pollution. How to maintain yield, but decrease pollution?

5   Biofortification: grow a diverse mix of crops or biofortification of staple crops to increase their nutritional status?

6   Biodiversity conservation strategies: conserving biodiversity within agricultural landscapes (land sharing) or concentrating production on the land devoted to it (land sparing)?

One area of real struggle is the debate between those who see globalised free markets as the way forward and those who are striving for localism. There are many people who would prefer more localised, low-input, non-industrialised agriculture, because it has much less impact on the environment. Locally grown food is definitely becoming very popular in the UK, as is clear from the high demand for allotments and the popularity of farmers' markets. Some questions to consider: can we keep going with globalised agriculture in the face of environmental degradation? If not can localism feed the growing world population? Is there any sensible middle way between the two ideologies? We do not have the answers, but they are important questions.

It is clear that there is major disagreement on the best way forward for food production, and nowhere is the disagreement more intense than with our next topic.

Genetically modified crops

As a plant scientist, I (Martin) not infrequently get asked to talk about GM crops. In summer 2010, I was very pleased to be invited to speak at the House of Commons in London. The meeting was on GM crops and food security 2010–2050, and it was arranged by the Associate Parliamentary Food and Health Forum.[9] I was given the title 'Are GM crops necessary to secure global food supplies at affordable prices?' The organisers specifically asked if I could give a balanced presentation, which I always try to do anyway. It was an interesting experience, and

I could see why they wanted balance, as two of the other speakers represented fairly extreme pro- and anti- positions. I have twice written on GM crops, once in a popular[10] and once in a more academic[11] context. It therefore seems unnecessary to reiterate all my thinking on GM crops in great detail. In brief, I have some concerns about moving genes between totally unrelated species, I have fewer worries about food safety than many, and there are some environmental problems with GM crops, but these are probably not insurmountable. The area where I have my greatest concern has little to do with science and more to do with politics, economics and globalisation. Who owns GM crops, and what are their motivations?

Let us begin with some statistics. In 2016, German pharmaceutical company Bayer succeeded in a $66 billion takeover bid of Monsanto. Bayer now controls 29 per cent of the global seed market and 24 per cent of the global pesticide market.[12] In 2018 four big agrochemical/ seed firms controlled over 60 per cent of the world's seeds: Bayer; BASF; Chemchina; and Corteva, the product of a merger between Dow and Dupont.[13] The United States Department of Agriculture (USDA) reported in 2020 that over 90 per cent of maize (sweetcorn), cotton and soybean grown in the United States was GM.[14] It is these kinds of figures that worry many people.

At present most GM crops are grown in six countries, and hardly any are grown in Europe. Only a limited number of crop species are GM, and at the moment there is no GM wheat grown commercially in the world. By far the dominant modifications are for herbicide resistance and insect resistance, and most GM crops are not grown for human consumption. However, the big concern for many in the world development and environmental movements is that large multinational companies might eventually take over much of the food chain. This idea is not restricted to GM crops, and as we have seen much non-GM agriculture is controlled by large companies. GM technologies seem to offer greater prospects for corporate control for two reasons: linked products and patents. So, with herbicide resistant crops, farmers have to buy the herbicide from the same company that they buy their seed from. Patents enable companies to prevent farmers from keeping seed to sow the next year, or from growing seed from other sources that contains 'their genes'.

This is a very rapidly developing area. Since the first edition of our book in 2015, we have seen the new technique of genome editing coming much to the fore. In 'traditional' GM crops, quite large sections of genetic material were transferred from one organism to another. With genome editing the process is much more precise and targeted. It is possible to change a very small part of the plant genome without introducing material from other organisms. Many of the objections to GM crops are overcome, but of course the economic and globalisation problems remain.

In the UK there has not been a lot of interest in GM crops for some years, and the topic has rarely made the news. However, this may well change with the UK leaving the European Union. The EU has pursued policies that have meant very little GM crops have been grown in Europe, and GM products are rarely seen in shops. When the UK leaves the EU in 2021 it may well wish to increase trade with the United States, which would undoubtedly increase pressure to allow GM products into the country and possibly to grow GM crops.

How can food science help?

One of Martin's former colleagues, now at the University of Nottingham, is Andrew Rosenthal. Here Andrew tells us how he became interested in food science and recounts some of his experience:

My father's childhood sweetheart married Harry, who later became professor of food science, yet was always a family friend. While growing up, we would chat about food and my interest in the subject flourished. After graduating I was convinced that single cell protein was the answer to world hunger. Forty years on, it has lost its appeal and insect protein seems to have taken its place as the vogue solution for reducing the west's overconsumption of meat. While alternative proteins may have a place in solving inequalities of food distribution, issues of malnutrition are as much political as scientific or technological.

What science and technology can help us with is understanding factors that control the quality of foods. By manipulating such factors, we can extend the shelf-life of foods providing a varied diet, with produce available out of season or non-indigenous crops to choose from. While food preservation does not sound as 'sexy' as ending world hunger, in practical terms it can improve the quality of what we all eat and can help poor farmers in the developing world eke out a living. Underlying the scientific approach are instruments and procedures to measure the quality attributes of materials throughout production.

Of course, good-quality food existed before a scientific approach was taken; master bakers, cheesemakers and brewers, along with chefs and other master craftspeople, have an excellent understanding of what makes a good product. These artisanal origins continue today with some manufacturing industries (e.g. tea or whisky blending). Yet food science has given us new ingredients and new processes to help extend shelf life and create innovative products. Moreover we have improved ways to control large-scale industrial processes and to measure quality. Industrialisation and its associated economy of scale has tended to centralise food manufacture, making the location of the factory key for raw material transport and product distribution.

Some years ago I visited a project in Sri Lanka coordinated by the Intermediate Technology Development Group.[15] The problem had been that tomato farmers experienced crush damage of fruit on route to market. Such damage resulted in loss of product quality along with loss of value. The solution offered was to set up a farmers' cooperative and process the tomatoes into a spicy tomato sauce close to the point of cultivation. The outcome was a reduction in losses and added value for the small farmers who ended up selling a shelf-life stable sauce. Bizarrely, one of the avenues currently being explored by the multinational food companies is distributed manufacturing, whereby modularised container-based mini-factories can be offloaded from a truck and used to process a product at the point of production in remote communities.

In the west, wheat is our staple food, providing the bulk of our energy through products like pasta and bread. We are told that Jesus fed 5,000 people on a few loaves. What quality of bread do you imagine God would miraculously create? I rather imagine it is not an inexpensive/budget/essential range.

Plant-based diets

Every restaurant and every food shop now seem to have vegan options, whether it's a sausage roll, a carton of oat milk or a quinoa salad. Plant-based diets are on the rise, and it has been interesting to see food culture change.[16]

There have been three main factors driving this. These diets can be healthier, with lots of fresh vegetables and fruit. There are some basic minerals and vitamins that are harder to gain from plants alone, but overall eating a plant-based diet is usually healthy. This is not the only reason why people choose this option. People are also concerned about animal welfare. What sort of lives and deaths are experienced by animals raised for meat? Should we even consider keeping and killing sentient animals for food? Along with animal welfare, people have concerns about the environment. Animals take up a lot of land and eat cereal crops that could be used to feed humans directly. Human population is over four times greater than a century ago, and the increase in domestic animals will have more than matched that. This has had a damaging impact on biodiversity, and livestock farming contributes to climate change through production of methane from animals (cattle and sheep) and in the clearing of forests for pasture and feed crops. Our world's fish stocks are in severe decline and huge trawlers take massive catches out of the sea at unsustainable levels.

It is for all these reasons that people have been switching away from diets where meat is a primary staple. Some choose a vegan diet and avoid all food of animal origin. Others have chosen to go vegetarian (including dairy and eggs) or flexitarian (where meat and fish from sustainable sources are eaten as a treat rather than as a staple). Whatever the balance of diet, the best way to eat sustainably is to buy food from producers and shops who are concerned about the environment, animal welfare and fair trade.

Experiences in Southall and Hayes

We began this chapter by looking at Pitres in Spain, a village with a fair degree of localism, and we will now return to localism. Kailean and Kim Khongsai are from India and are CMS mission partners serving with A Rocha UK, based in Southall, west London. Kailean is the A Rocha UK community manager, and here he describes some of his work:

In my search for a feasible environmental project that could attract the local community in Southall and Hayes, I have met and interacted with people from various faith and cultural backgrounds. On many occasions my questions on environmental topics have been diverted or ignored. I still remember one person saying, 'Climate change and conservation science are too complex for me, and I would rather sit back and plant some tomatoes for my kitchen.' This did not surprise me much as the area is known to suffer from a lack of environmental understanding and engagement, and people find it hard to relate to what I do. The only way to get people's attention and to set them thinking about environmental issues was to talk about food. This is something they can relate to, especially the Asians and Caribbeans who love food and spices so much.

Since then, I have started organising events related to food. These would be associated with other activities like a walk in the park, picking berries and helping people identify native trees, birds and wildflowers. They have received a good response from the community. For me, food became the key to open doors for spreading environmental awareness, encouraging people and mobilising local resources (for example, finding volunteers, borrowing tools and equipment). I realised from this experience that people are more drawn and connected to the things they are familiar with and have already experienced. Having learned that lesson, I applied it to Bixley Fields community garden in 2010 and later to Wolf Fields nature reserve, after A Rocha UK acquired the site in 2013.[17] We started a project with a small food-growing plot and later installed a sensory garden, wildlife pond, wildflower meadow and an orchard supported by the apiary. These additions had a noticeable impact on the site's species diversity. It also provides an opportunity for outdoor education, environmental stewardship, promoting an active lifestyle and healthy eating.

In these projects, we work closely with local authorities, churches, schools and residents. Involving people in doing something practical is not always easy. But a simple 'bring and share' meal or coffee morning does bring people together. This stimulates social interaction, provides space to encourage one another and brings about local commitment to doing something positive.

Biblical reflection: Incarnation

Kailean's work for A Rocha UK has encouraged community interaction and enabled community engagement with the local environment. Churches seeking to reach out to their communities may find new energy through understanding more of the link between the Christian faith and environmental community action. A key doctrine is that of incarnation, with Christ coming among us as a human being.

Miracle at midnight

Taking midnight services on Christmas Eve is always a joy, especially in small country churches. For a few years Margot was Chaplain of Jesus College, Oxford, and at Christmas time used to help her brother, Mike, who was vicar of six churches in Somerset. One Christmas, we went to the tiny church of Sutton Montis, set in the hills near Cadbury Castle. We drove up through the hills and arrived in the village, which was lit only from a few chinks of Christmas lights peeping through the curtains of the houses. We parked in the churchwarden's farm opposite the church and walked up the dark path, glimpsing through the shadows the amazing view across the Somerset Levels. As we entered the church we met a burst of light. The golden limestone glowed with candles and Christmas decorations, and church members gave us a warm welcome. We had a wonderful service with a packed church, the miracle of the birth of Christ coming afresh to us all.

The churchwarden walked us back to our car, but first took us aside in the farmyard to open the top of a stable door. We peered inside to see a ewe with two new-born lambs. We looked on in a magical, holy silence. In that moment we met with Jesus, born among shepherds and animals; son of our loving father God who knows when every creature gives birth (Job 39:1).

Jesus, incarnation and creation

The gospel read that evening was the classic midnight passage, John 1. This has become a key passage to understand about how God, creation, humans and God's mission all interact. God's covenant was revealed in a way that had never happened before. In John 1 we see the divinity of Christ and the humanity of Christ intrinsically interconnected. We have arrived at the intersection where the divine and the material cleave together. The relationships in the Trinity have been made visible in God's interrelationships with creation and humanity.

God's mission on Earth fully springs into action. It heralds the advent of new creation.

In first-century Palestine, Hebrew and Greek ideas jostled together. John, when reflecting on Jesus, took the concept of *logos*, which means both 'word' and 'wisdom'. *Logos* was used in the Greek translation of Proverbs 8 for a personified wisdom who calls people to understanding and justice. John, in an inspired masterstroke of theology and poetry, sees in Genesis 1 both the first expression of Christ, as God speaks to bring creation into being, and the fulfilment of wisdom in the Word.

The Word has always existed. He was there in eternity, outside of creation. At the start of John, the camera lens has been drawn back. We find ourselves glimpsing into eternity, before the universe was created. Here we see the intimate relationships between Father, Son and Holy Spirit. Simultaneously with this eternal view of Christ, John takes us into creation. The phrase translated 'In the beginning' evokes the start of Genesis 1. Creation is described as 'all things' (John 1:3) and by the Greek word 'cosmos' (John 1:9–10). Richard Bauckham explains that 'all things' means the whole of creation, the universe. 'Cosmos' changes its meaning. It usually meant the 'world beneath the sky' and this is the meaning in verse 9; however, by the last reference in verse 10, it is more likely referring to humanity. As the gospel unfolds, whatever the primary meaning of 'cosmos', there is always 'a reminder that humans are part of a wider creation'.[18]

In John 1, we reach the climax to the passage in verse 14: 'the Word became flesh and made his dwelling among us'. John Haught writes, 'Rather than dwelling in a platonic sanctuary above the terrors of history, the God of Christianity became embodied in events that are historically and culturally contingent.'[19] God came into his own material world in a specific place and at a specific time, and in doing so hallowed all places for all time. This is God's embodiment of his love for his whole creation.

Incarnation and localism

The incarnation is not so much about 'how Jesus can be both human and divine but about how he exists in relationship'.[20] The implication for creation is a recovery of lost relationships between God, humanity and nature. This is not simply in a cosmic sense, but in our ordinary everyday contexts. To follow Christ fully we need to acknowledge that he was born in a real place and time. His birth may have been in a stable or a family room next to the animals. In our imaginations we smell the fresh hay, feel the warmth of the animals and hear the muffled voices of the shepherds. To follow Christ fully we need to engage with our own local surroundings and find something in them to value. Adrian Hough believes that rural churches at their best do this, almost without realising it. They engage with the community around them. The church in that case is not simply an 'it' but belongs to that community.[21] Local churches in other situations can have similar potential.

Modern life, urban and rural, can be disconnected from a locality, however. To recover the sense of belonging, we fill our homes with possessions. Contentment becomes a never fulfilled dream. As soon as one prize is gained, we reach out for another. Through understanding incarnation we can discover our sense of belonging within the relationships we have in our locality. These relationships are with God, people and place. This is not anti-material but a rediscovery of the joy and value of things that reflect those relationships. Our experience on sabbatical in the mountain village of Pitres was one of relationship. Even without great Spanish, we got to know local people and bought local produce. For a few weeks, we belonged.

When we first arrived in Haddenham, a wonderful food hamper awaited us with a huge chocolate cake on the top! It astonished the removal men, who for a moment dropped their 'Vicar of Dibley' banter and became quite serious. They said, 'It's real, isn't it?' That hamper did more for the incarnation of Jesus in the lives of those men than any sermons or services. In the hamper were two beautiful mugs that we use almost every day. They are a great reminder of the care of our church members for us and of God's love for everyone.

Building a community with cake

Down the road from Haddenham is the village of Kingsey with one of the loveliest Victorian churches in the country. Kingsey had a thriving community in the 20th century but by 2010 the congregation was thinner on the ground and the community was struggling. The older folk had died or moved to larger villages. Younger families had moved in, but with only the church and a busy main road, the new people had not mixed in the same way. Out of all of this was born the Kingsey Breakfast – a monthly breakfast in the church with a very short all-age service at the end. Amazing coffee, bacon sandwiches, muffins and more were laid on each month and the whole of Kingsey began to come along (and were soon signed up on the rota to help with breakfast). As people became friends, other events followed. The village fete had started to struggle for volunteers and now sprung back into life. It was held at Tythrop, a stunning manor house owned by a successful business couple. They offered the church members a project to provide teas for the open garden days at the manor. Soon cakes were being baked by the oven full and teams were assembled for the various tasks (washing up was the most hilarious with much ribbing of one another). Kingsey church had always had finances a little in the red but had somehow made it year to year. As the cakes started to flow, so the church became solvent again. PCC (church council) meetings were happy evenings, full of laughter and new plans. The church ran an ambitious open church project to restore a beautiful Victorian altar frontal – more cake and many more people. Bonfire night (bangers in buns), Hymns and Pimms (home-smoked salmon) and other events followed. There were no long sermons and prayers were very simple but the Holy Spirit revealed the love of God in Kingsey Church. You'll not see much on the outside if you drive through Kingsey and you could easily miss it, but Kingsey has huge heart and a wonderful community – full of cake!

Incarnation and food

If we need to recover a relationship with our local place and community, we also need to recover a relationship with our food. Martin
and I have never been brilliant at growing food, but there is something amazing about eating food you have grown. When we moved
into our new vicarage in 2019 we not only had a large garden around
the house but an adjacent vegetable patch that was more like a field.
We prepared some beds and bought seeds and seedlings to see if we
could grow things. Not everything survived but the evening we ate our
own cauliflower cheese with our own baked potatoes felt especially
good. Even if you don't grow food, many people in the UK find it more
satisfying to buy and eat something that has been grown locally. It's
interesting that some supermarkets now have pictures of the farm
where meat was sourced with a description of how the animals were
reared. Martin has already explored the dilemma between local food
and bulk production. Whatever the conclusion, having some local food
increases connections to our community. In West Oxfordshire we are
on the mailing list of two nearby farms that produce high welfare
organic and Pasture for Life Certified meat. We are flexitarian, eating vegetarian or vegan for most meals but have meat about once a
week and a box from these farms every couple of months is just right
for us. It is more expensive than meat from a supermarket but our
plant-based meals are cheaper and so it evens out. There is a local
market garden that supplies organic veg and fruit boxes and we get
honey from our local farmer. The community shop in our village buys
from a local market, baker and butcher. During spring 2020 it supplied
all those who were shielding with boxes of groceries. We live in the
country and it is easy for us to find local food, but it is also possible in
cities and many veg box schemes deliver into urban areas.

Food banks

All these things are very good, but for some folk any decent food is a
luxury. In the UK there are significant numbers of people who struggle

to feed their families. Food banks have been established in response to this need. The Trussell Trust is the largest organisation running UK food banks, and most of them are hosted by churches.[22] Between 1 April 2019 and 31 March 2020, Trussell food banks distributed 1.9 million three-day emergency food supplies to people in crisis, from 1,200 food banks around the UK. Of these people over 700,000 were children (this is double the figures in the first edition of this book in 2015 and triple the number of food banks). Trussell work on a referral system and the main reasons for these referrals were low income, benefit delays and changes in benefits. In April 2020 there was an 89 per cent surge in demand as the Covid-19 lockdown began. This is likely to translate into a significant long-term increase in the need for food banks as recession inevitably follows the pandemic. There also is a major problem with hunger worldwide and this will be a focus of our next chapter.

Food-growing with A Rocha UK

What about food-growing in the inner city? Kailean Khongsai writes about his involvement in supporting food-growing in Southall:

> Our food-growing projects in Southall are witnessing a real success in terms of engaging the local communities from various ethnic and faith backgrounds. It was a slow start which took several 'meetings and light snacks' with faith groups and community leaders to foster local interest and commitment to environmental action. Investing time in building relationships and identifying local issues has been very fruitful longer-term.
>
> Ever since the Wolf Fields project was launched, the site has attracted many people especially from low-income families. The project gives them the opportunity to gain new skills, and access to fresh vegetables and fruits. We grow together and celebrate, and share produce. We organised activities for both adults and children. This approach of combining fun and food activities is well received. The project offered an incredible space for

physical and mental healing and recovery and is now under the social prescribing scheme, allowing local GPs to refer patients for non-clinical services. In addition, the site became an excellent learning place for the youth and local primary schools with over a 1,000 children visiting annually. The site also provides valuable habitats for local wildlife, and plays a crucial role in regenerating a derelict land and its neighbourhoods.

'I am so pleased that this unpleasant and dreadful site has become a wonderful place to relax and enjoy wildlife and meet new people' (Elizabeth, a local resident).

'We harvest not just vegetables, but also friendships, fun and love' (Pardeep, another local resident).

Taking bread and wine

One of the features of our Haddenham vicarage was a large grapevine climbing up the wall. For a number of years Tim, a former church-warden, took our grapes and turned them into wonderful rosé wine. Jesus' embodiment of covenant came to a climax with the bread and wine at the last supper (Mark 14:22–26). It was the night before he died and the time of the Passover festival, when Jewish people were celebrating their escape from Egypt. The bread is a reminder of the manna God provided in the wilderness, and of God's provision for us through the natural world (see chapter 3). Jesus, in calling his disciples to take the bread as his body, was acknowledging his incarnation: he became part of creation for the love of his world. In breaking the bread, he was foreshadowing the cross and the salvation to come. As he took the cup of wine, Jesus described it as his blood of the covenant. Noah was commanded not to eat the lifeblood of animals (Genesis 9:4), and Richard Bauckham sees this as acknowledging the sacredness of life.[23] Jesus invites us into the sacredness of his salvation, won through the pouring out of his lifeblood for atonement. Giving the cup to his disciples, Jesus said that he will next drink it in the kingdom of God. Jesus lifted the eyes of his disciples and offered them a view of the kingdom to come, when the covenant will be complete and all creation will be reconciled 'by making peace through his blood, shed on the cross' (Colossians 1:20).

Food, incarnation and relationship

The recurring theme of this chapter has been that of relationship. We have seen this in the tension between localism and globalisation, and we have been reminded that we are dependent on the Earth for food and our very existence. The incarnation is supremely about relationship. God announces a new covenant and points towards the healing of our relationships with him, each other and the Earth. One way we begin to work this out is in how we grow, buy and eat food. In Communion our covenant bonds are crystallised as we encounter and remember the Word made flesh, bringing wisdom, justice and love. Let us work to bring these values to the future management of our food at global and local levels.

 ECO TIP Take a food item you normally discard and see if you can turn it into a delicious meal. Here is a recipe to give you an idea.

CAULIFLOWER STALK SOUP (serves four)

Stalks, base and leaves
  of a cauliflower, chopped
100 g red lentils
one onion, chopped

oil
garlic, chopped (optional)
boiling water
tinned coconut milk

Heat the oil in a pan then sauté the onion and garlic. Add the cauliflower and cook gently for a few minutes. Add the lentils and enough boiling water to cover. Boil for a few minutes and then simmer for about 20 minutes until the lentils are cooked, adding more water if needed. Add the coconut and heat through. Lightly purée to serve. Using more lentils will produce a dhal that can be served with rice or naan bread.

Bible study: loaves, fishes and the bread of life

Read John 6:1–15

1 Which part of this story do you like most and why?
2 What does it say about the creator and his creation?
3 What are the motives of the different people in the story and what does this say about them?

Read: John 6:30–40

4 Why did people point to manna in asking Jesus for a sign that he came from God?
5 How does the bread of life connect both to this Earth and to eternity?
6 How does this link to resurrection?

Notes

1 La Oveja Verde, **laovejaverde.es** (accessed 21 August 2020).
2 FAO, 'Food security', *FAO Policy Brief* 2 (June 2006), **fao.org/ fileadmin/templates/faoitaly/documents/pdf/pdf_Food_Security_ Cocept_Note.pdf** (accessed 19 August 2020).
3 'World hunger: key facts and statistics 2020' **actionagainsthunger. org/world-hunger-facts-statistics** (accessed 19 August 2020).
4 H. Ritchie and M. Roser, 'Crop yields', **ourworldindata.org/ crop-yields** (accessed 19 August 2020).
5 The Royal Society, 'Reaping the Benefits: science and the sustainable intensification of global agriculture', *RS Policy document* 11, no. 9 (2009), p. 46.
6 B.D. McIntyre et al. (eds), 'International Assessment of Agricultural Knowledge, Science and Technology for Development (IAASTD)', synthesis report with executive summary – a synthesis of the global and sub-global IAASTD reports, 2009.
7 McIntyre et al., 'IAASTD', p. 45.

8   HLPE, 'Agroecological and other innovative approaches for sustainable agriculture and food systems that enhance food security and nutrition', report by the High Level Panel of Experts on Food Security and Nutrition of the Committee on World Food Security, 2019, Rome.

9   M.J. Hodson, 'Are GM crops necessary to secure global food supplies at affordable prices?', presentation to GM Crops and Food Security 2010–2050, Associate Parliamentary Food and Health Forum, House of Commons, London, 2010, **hodsons.org/MartinHodson/GMcropsFHF2010.pdf** (accessed 19 August 2020).

10   Hodson and Hodson, *Cherishing the Earth*, pp. 182–88.

11   M.J. Hodson and J.A. Bryant, *Functional Biology of Plants* (Wiley-Blackwell, 2012), pp. 297–300.

12   C. Smaller, 'Bayer tightens control over the world's food supply', *IISD blog*, 23 September 2016, **iisd.org/articles/bayer-tightens-control-over-worlds-food-supply** (accessed 19 August 2020).

13   P.H. Howard, 'Global seed industry changes since 2013', 31 December 2018, **philhoward.net/2018/12/31/global-seed-industry-changes-since-2013** (accessed 19 August 2020).

14   'Recent trends in GE adoption', **ers.usda.gov/data-products/adoption-of-genetically-engineered-crops-in-the-us/recent-trends-in-ge-adoption.aspx** (accessed 19 August 2020).

15   The Intermediate Technology Development Group is now called Practical Action and can be found at **practicalaction.org** (accessed 27 August 2020).

16   For more on this topic see M. Smith, *The Plant-based Diet: A Christian option?* (Grove Books, 2019).

17   A Rocha UK, Wolf Fields, Southall, **arocha.org.uk/our-activities/practical-conservation/wolf-fields** (accessed 14 June 2020)

18   Bauckham, *Bible and Ecology*, p. 163.

19   J.F. Haught, *God and the New Atheism* (Westminster John Knox, 2008), p. 102.

20   A. Hough, 'Rural church and environmental crisis: incarnational response in an age of global change', *Rural Theology* 10 (2012), pp. 43–55.

21   Hough, 'Rural church and environmental crisis'.

22   The Trussell Trust, **trusselltrust.org** (accessed 27 September 2020).

23   Bauckham, *Bible and Ecology*, p. 119.

ENVIRONMENT AND SUSTAINABLE DEVELOPMENT

Berchules, tomatoes and migrant workers

One day on our sabbatical in Spain we travelled east from our base in Pitres to Berchules, a small village in a more remote part of the Sierra Nevada. We intended to walk out from there up into the valley to the north. Before we set out we had a coffee outside a bar in the plaza, and while we were drinking it several African men walked past. We wondered quite why they were in this rather off the beaten track sort of place. The walk from Berchules was very pleasant, following *acequias* for most of the way. Then, in the distance, we spotted some sort of agricultural activity. As we drew closer we saw fields of vine tomatoes being harvested by several African men. The tomato fields had evidently expanded recently and our (relatively new) walking guidebook was now out of date, as there were so many new fields of tomatoes. At one point this meant crawling under a fence that had not been there when the guidebook was written, but we made it back to Berchules with no major problems and had a cold drink at the bar. We made a mental note to find out more about the tomatoes and the migrant workers of Berchules.

It seems the area has always been known for tomatoes, which grow well there, and at that altitude suffer from fewer pest species. Since the financial crisis of 2008, people who used to work in the cities have returned to the village, having lost their jobs.[1] Some owned land that had belonged to their parents, and they decided to grow tomatoes for export to Germany. So this activity tripled in three years. To look after and harvest all the extra fields of tomatoes needed a labour force, hence the African migrant workers. They come from North and sub-Saharan Africa and are employed in the extensive greenhouses of Andalucía, moving out into the fields in the summer. In Berchules the migrant workers live in a camp outside the village, having made often difficult journeys from their homelands to escape famine, war and poor job prospects.[2]

We have no evidence to suggest that the African workers in Berchules were in any way unhappy or being exploited. However, in 2011 *The Guardian* ran an article in which it was claimed that many migrant workers in Andalucía were living and working in terrible conditions, and being paid very poorly.[3] It is not known how many migrant workers there are in Andalucía as many are illegal immigrants, but in 2010 the estimate was 80,000–90,000, and the evidence suggests that many more have come since. The Andalusian horticulture industry was not happy with the article and said that their operations were audited both by the local authorities and by the international companies purchasing the vegetables.[4] However, reports continue to circulate about poor conditions for migrant workers in Spain. In March 2020, as the Covid-19 pandemic hit southern Spain, charities and campaign groups suggested that workers were not able to adequately protect themselves from the virus.[5]

Our decision to take a walk from Berchules surprisingly led us into the whole area of human migration. It is of course already a controversial topic in many parts of the world, including Europe. We have to wonder what will happen if the population of Africa does rise to three billion (chapter 5), and if rapid climate change occurs during this century. Will we be welcoming to migrants? Will we even become migrants ourselves?

A global perspective on environment and sustainable development

In the past, concern for the environment and concern for the world's poorest people were seen to some extent as separate issues, or even issues that were in conflict with each other. That kind of thinking has now largely gone. Environmental issues, and particularly climate change, are seen as being of key importance to world development and to the future of the poor. The UN introduced the Millennium Development Goals (MDGs) in 2000, and they ran for 15 years. Although the MDGs were good goals to have, they still reflected a lack of understanding of the interconnectedness between human and environmental concerns, and also had no goal to reduce the human birth rate. The MDGs expired, and the UN released its last report on them in 2015.[6] In many areas considerable progress had been made. The number of people living in extreme poverty had more than halved, fewer people were hungry or malnourished, and more people had access to safe drinking water. Also, malaria, measles, tuberculosis and AIDS were under better control. A number of other goals were less on target, including those for child survival, maternal deaths and education. However, both climate change and biodiversity loss remained very serious issues as we saw in chapters 2 and 3. The problem identified was that our environmental unsustainability could eventually send the progress made on the other MDGs spinning into reverse. Looking forward to the era after the MDGs, the UN had this to say on environmental sustainability:

> One theme emerging from the debate on the successor agenda to the MDGs is the importance of true integration of environment into development ambitions. Environmental sustainability is a core pillar of the post-2015 agenda and a prerequisite for lasting socioeconomic development and poverty eradication.

The Sustainable Development Goals (SDGs)[7] were presented to a special session of the UN General Assembly in September 2015 and launched in 2016. They are intended to be achieved by 2030. The 17

SDGs are: no poverty; zero hunger; good health and well-being; quality education; gender equality; clean water and sanitation; affordable and clean energy; decent work and economic growth; industry, innovation, and infrastructure; reducing inequality; sustainable cities and communities; responsible consumption and production; climate action; life below water; life on land; peace, justice and strong institutions; and partnerships for the goals. So we have gone from 8 MDGs to 17 SDGs. Moreover within the 17 SDGs there are 169 targets. The year the targets are supposed to be achieved varies between 2020 and 2030, and some have no end date. Not surprisingly there have been criticisms that there are too many SDGs and targets, and that the whole system is too complex. However, only one of the MDGs (the seventh, 'Ensure environmental sustainability') concerned the environment, while seven SDGs have at least some environmental focus. So at least on paper there is more emphasis on environmental sustainability than was previously the case. Another key difference was that the MDGs were intended to apply mostly to developing countries, while the SDGs are designed to be applied to all countries.

What progress has been made in achieving the SDGs?[8] Even before the Covid-19 pandemic hit, progress had been patchy: in some areas, such as the incidence of many diseases and access to drinking water, there had been improvements, but the decline in the natural environment had been continuing at an alarming rate. When the pandemic did hit, however, it threatened to totally undermine much of this progress. The UN report of 2020 contains an overview section with a series of alarming graphics illustrating the widespread impact of Covid-19. Just a few of the headlines show the scale of the problem: an additional 71 million people were pushed into extreme poverty in 2020; the pandemic is an additional threat to food systems; only 65 per cent of primary schools have basic handwashing facilities critical for Covid-19 prevention; and the most vulnerable groups are being hit hardest by the pandemic. There were a few positives, like decreased carbon emissions during the lockdowns, but overall the outlook was bleak. António Guterres, the secretary general of the UN, wrote in his foreword to the report:

Far from undermining the case for the SDGs, the root causes and uneven impacts of Covid-19 demonstrate precisely why we need the 2030 Agenda, the Paris Agreement on climate change and the Addis Ababa Action Agenda, and underscore the urgency of their implementation. I have therefore consistently called for a coordinated and comprehensive international response and recovery effort, based on sound data and science and guided by the sustainable development goals.

In September 2020, the Bill and Melinda Gates Foundation released their latest Goalkeepers report.[9] Their conclusions were stark: after 20 years of continually declining, the pandemic had thrown millions more people into extreme poverty, vaccine coverage for other diseases was down to levels last seen in the 1990s and globally inequalities were rising.

Into the doughnut

How do we provide a setting in which humanity can flourish without making the environmental crisis even worse? How do we balance human need with caring for the natural world? How do we change our current economic model to something that will work in this century? Kate Raworth, an economist at Oxford University, has attempted to find some answers to these questions in her 2017 book *Doughnut Economics*.[10]

Think of a doughnut. Around the outside edge place the nine planetary boundaries we met in chapter 1 (table 1, column 4). These are the outer boundaries beyond which we might damage the integrity of the biosphere and make the planet uninhabitable for humans and much of our biodiversity. On the inner edge of the doughnut, Raworth places twelve social dimensions that are derived from the SDGs: food; health; education; income and work; water and sanitation; energy; networks; housing; gender equality; social equity; political voice; and peace and justice. These represent a 'social foundation of well-being that no one should fall below'. Raworth says we need to find the 'sweet spot' in the doughnut where all human needs are met without damaging our planet.

How to do this? She considers that we need to radically change our economic model. This involves moving our focus away from gross domestic product and endless economic growth towards thriving in balance. Crucially, Raworth suggests that the environment should no longer be seen as an 'externality', an item outside the economic model. For example, typically pollution produced by an industry was seen as an externality and not as a cost to that industry; hence the need for regulation. But, Raworth argues, we need more than regulation, as pollution (e.g. carbon emissions) should be included as part of the new economic model.

Doughnut Economics is a somewhat controversial book in economics circles. Whether it will lead to changes in the teaching of economics at universities or to changes in government policies that will move us towards sustainable development remains to be seen.

Climate stewards and offsetting

In chapter 6 we heard from Caroline Pomeroy about her carbon footprint calculator in one part of her work as director of Climate Stewards.[11] The other half of Caroline's work draws on her experience working in Africa and on climate change. She writes:

> Whatever part of the world we live in and whatever our situation, dealing with climate change must involve both mitigation and adaptation. Mitigation means adopting strategies and techniques which will reduce greenhouse gas emissions and/ or reduce the amount of fossil fuel we consume. Adaptation involves coping with the effects of climate change. Climate Stewards' work embodies both mitigation and adaptation, while at the same time tackling rural poverty and creating more sustainable, resilient communities.

Through our local partners (mostly church-based organisations) in Ghana, Kenya, Uganda and Tanzania, we plant
indigenous trees with churches, schools and communities.
This work brings triple benefits. The new trees sequester
carbon dioxide, removing it from the atmosphere (a global 'commons')[12] and locking it up as carbon in the trees (*mitigation*).
Local biodiversity is enhanced, flood risk is reduced, soils are
conserved and the micro-climate improves as new forest areas
are created (*adaptation*). Churches, schools and communities
benefit from sustainable forest products such as seeds and fruit
in the medium term, and thinnings and timber in the longer term
(*sustainable development*). Meanwhile, churches and schools
teach people about the theology of creation care and the skills
they need to put this into practice.

Climate Stewards' projects are carefully designed to ensure
permanence, *additionality* and no *leakage*. Permanence means
that the trees will survive in the long term, and it is achieved
by strong community engagement and education. Additionality means that the tree planting (or other intervention) would
not have happened without Climate Stewards' support. Our
schemes are also designed to prevent leakage – we ensure that
planting trees in one area does not lead to farmers cutting trees
down elsewhere.

In Uganda, Nepal and Peru, our partners train and equip
families with water filters, cookstoves and fireless cookers.
These intermediate technologies all reduce consumption of
firewood and charcoal, thus reducing pressure on remaining
forests, while helping households to save money and improve
health through reduction of smoke in the house. Each project is
carefully designed to ensure that it is fully 'owned' by the community, with families involved in construction and installation
of the stoves, and receiving training and support throughout
the life of the project.

All our projects are designed to meet the Climate Stewards
'Seal of Approval' standard, which requires accurate baseline

information, conservative estimates of carbon mitigation and regular monitoring.

With a UK government target of Net Zero by 2050 and a Church of England target of Net Zero by 2030, there is considerable pressure for us all to reduce carbon emissions year on year and to offset the rest. Climate Stewards encourages people and organisations to do exactly this; voluntary carbon offsetting is not a licence to pollute, but a responsible choice to deal with unavoidable carbon emissions. Using our online carbon calculator tools, businesses, churches, NGOs and individuals can calculate their emissions and pay to offset any combination of flights, land travel, energy, expenditure, food and waste. This offsetting income is used to fund our overseas projects, buying an equivalent quantity of carbon savings.

Biblical reflection: Resurrection

Mountain sunrise

One of the special features of the Alpujarra Mountains in Spain is amazing sunrises. Every day is different. It all depends on the amount of cloud, the time of year and other factors such as dust in the atmosphere from the southern Saharan winds. The autumn sunrises are especially stunning. The sun announces its arrival with a changing pink and golden backdrop over the mountain range. By the time it appears the whole sky can be alight with fire.

It is surely no coincidence that the resurrection of Jesus was discovered at sunrise. As dawn announced the coming of a new day, so the loyal women followers of Jesus met him once more, this time in his resurrection body. They had kept vigil at the foot of the cross, seen life torn from him, minute by minute, hour by hour, reached the depths of their own despair and watched powerlessly as two powerful men took him and laid him in a tomb. We hope they knew it was a gentle act. They went home to prepare spices and returned on Easter Sunday to anoint his body and prepare it properly for burial. These women were not faint-hearted! As the dawn began to rise over Jerusalem, setting the sky ablaze, creation was recreated and Earth and sky rejoiced.

Resurrection and re-creation

Theologian N.T. Wright gives a persuasive account of the bodily resurrection of Christ.[13] In Judaism in the first century AD, there was a belief in resurrection for those who had held true to God. This belief came from continued longing for a full and proper restoration of Israel from exile and a renewal of covenant relationships. The prophecy of the dry bones in Ezekiel 37 was a promise of restoration but also a metaphor for resurrection. By the first century, there were many variations on what would happen. The overall idea was that, at death, a faithful person's soul would be kept safe with God, pending the final resurrection when they would be raised to enjoy God's new creation. As with the dry bones, a new body would be given and the covenant would be renewed and restored. This redeemed world would resemble that of Isaiah 11 and 65:17–25, with peace on Earth and restored harmony between God, people and creation.

This belief in the soul provided a worldview and a vocabulary that could have been drawn on to explain a merely spiritual or psychological encounter with Christ after his death. However, one of the overwhelming features of the early church was the insistence on the bodily resurrection of Christ (John 20:24–29; Luke 24:36–43). Given their understanding about souls, this insistence is extraordinary. Only a genuine resurrection would have led to such powerful accounts.

The implication of Jesus' resurrection was quickly understood by the disciples. Simply encountering Jesus' soul would have reassured them that he was safe with God but would not have changed the covenant landscape. With the rising of Christ, the covenant had been renewed and the new creation had been inaugurated. This new creation is not an entirely new universe, however. The resurrection of Jesus in the garden at Jerusalem means the new creation was inaugurated within this present creation. Resurrection hope is therefore fulfilled in a renewal of God's creation and not in its destruction. It is a hope that begins while the difficulties of the world remain with us.

It was fashionable a few decades ago for some Christians to believe that the resurrection was virtual rather than physical. This fitted with the intellectualised faith of the mid-20th century, but was weak in terms of empowering Christians to take practical action in the world. The belief that Jesus was indeed raised bodily forces the conclusion that this world is vitally important in God's purposes. As the resurrection marks the inauguration of God's new creation, the implication is that this new creation will culminate in a renewal of this Earth rather than an entirely new entity. The new covenant is therefore a renewing of the three-way covenant between God, the Earth (universe) and humans. We need to take our new-covenant partners seriously.

Creation groaning and redeemed

We see this understanding of the resurrection expanded in later New Testament passages. In Romans 8:18–26, Paul writes about creation groaning and waiting for the children of God to be revealed so that it can be brought into the freedom and glory. Creation is waiting for the final resurrection when creation itself will be renewed and restored and the children of God will have the joy of living in the new creation. Peter saw the final day of the Lord coming with fire to cleanse and lay bare the Earth (2 Peter 3:10). All that is not worthy will be destroyed but creation itself will be cleansed and renewed. We can now see how the resurrection of Christ culminates in the new creation in Revelation 21—22 (as discussed in chapter 4). All these texts were written in a context of suffering and difficulty but encourage readers in each generation to respond to suffering with courage, knowing of the hope that is to come (Romans 5:1–5; 1 Peter 4:12–19; Revelation 7:13–17).

Finally, the author of Hebrews wrote an inspired reflection on the relationship between God, creation, humans and redemption (Hebrews 1:1–4). He described Jesus as 'the radiance of God's glory' and 'heir of all things'. There are many resonances here with the cosmic passage about Christ in Colossians 1:15–20 (discussed in chapter 5). The writer to the Hebrews explains that Christ, who brought creation into being, has provided purification of sin and sustains all things through his powerful word. As we move from resurrection, through covenant renewal, to understanding Christ's sustaining of creation, we also realise that, as new-covenant Christians, we are the body of Christ and have a role in that sustaining process.[14]

Resurrection: connecting environment and sustainable development

We have seen that the resurrection of Jesus marked the beginning of new creation, and the renewal of the three-way covenant between God, people and the rest of the natural world. The implication for Christians is that we should make that covenant renewal a real part of our Christian discipleship. This means we should be concerned for both human suffering and environmental degradation as a core part of our Christian faith. These are signs of broken covenant relationships and we hold true to the power of the resurrection when we seek to restore these relationships to their proper life-giving harmony. We can help to mend those relationships in many different ways, but we need to use integrated approaches if we are truly pointing towards a restored and renewed world.

Susan Durber was Christian Aid's former theology advisor. She drew on biblical prophets and voices from the global south to make a just response to the impact of climate change on the poorest in the world.[15] Prophets not only critique and challenge society but also offer hope in a God who holds to his promises. They help us reimagine the future and find faith to bring that into being. The Archbishop of Southern Africa, Thabo Makgoba, writes movingly of this integrated approach in one of his poorest dioceses:

> Within my own Province, the poorest and most rural dioceses have been among the first to incorporate care for creation into their everyday life, and to integrate it holistically within the teaching of the Christian faith. One example from Lesotho was the decision that all baptism and confirmation candidates (or their families) plant a tree at their home, church or village. These are then seen as a symbol of faith, to be nurtured in the years ahead as they nurture their Christian commitment. This is increasingly becoming a very visible sign of witness within the local community, where deforestation and soil erosion are significant challenges.[16]

Archbishop Thabo encourages us to step back from unrealistic expectations of seeing a fully restored kingdom of God today, but to resist a fatalism that believes nothing can change. He observed the difficulties caused by both these approaches during apartheid and its aftermath. Overall, he encourages a redemptive engagement with creation.

Integral mission in action

In the past, human development and environmental conservation were wrongly seen as conflicting with each other. We have given strong practical arguments for an integrated approach, and we have also shown that this is more appropriate theologically for Christian action in our world. A Rocha Kenya has been particularly active in integral mission, and marine biologist Robert Sluka writes about their work on biodiversity conservation and development in marine protected areas:

> People or fish? Human development and flourishing versus biodiversity conservation is often presented as a zero-sum game. Yet research into the effectiveness of Marine Protected Areas (MPAs) suggests that by setting aside areas where fishing and other extractive activities are controlled, biodiversity can be protected and people will benefit as well. Fish grow larger in

these protected areas, and as egg production is exponentially related to size, the abundance of larger-sized individuals results in replenishment of fished areas.

A Rocha Kenya's Mwamba Field Study Centre is located on the shore of Watamu Marine National Park. We have focused on research that leads to better understanding and management of this marine park. In addition to beautiful coral reefs, habitats include sea-grass beds, beaches and intertidal rock pools. Our research into these rock pools revealed an East African endemic coral species and the presence of juveniles of many commercially important species.[17] These rock pools, then, serve as a nursery ground that supports species which grow and provide eggs or move out of the reserve to replenish the surrounding areas, which are utilised by coastal fishermen. There has been little focus in Christian communities on serving these usually poor coastal fishing communities, particularly in the Indian Ocean.[18]

A Rocha Kenya is involved in conservation projects that protect this amazing biodiversity, whose primary purpose is to glorify God. We are revealing the hidden things of God in the ocean.[19] Yet God is gracious and he also made it so that biodiversity provides for people. This happens in the MPA discussed above, but A Rocha Kenya has also been working with the local community to study the tourism industry and ways in which it can be more sustainable. This includes partnering with other local marine conservation organisations to evaluate the impacts of tourism on the coral reefs,[20] and training staff of tourist boats in best practices. We have recently discovered some dangerous practices by the unregulated and informal rock-pool tourism operators, which we are addressing. We are particularly trying to serve the local 'beach boys' who have very difficult lives and are often involved in this trade.

MPAs are not a panacea and they must be developed in conjunction with conservation in the surrounding waters and even on land, controlling, for example, runoff of pollution. However, MPAs resonate with a number of Christian principles, such as sabbath, resurrection and justice.[21] A thoroughly integrated, holistic Christian approach to marine conservation, utilising the best available science, theology and conservation practice provides hope for the ocean as well as for the people that depend on it throughout the world.

The powerful and powerless were faithful at the cross

It is significant that both the powerful and the powerless kept watch on Good Friday (John 19:25–27, 38–42; Mark 15:40–43). They were together in seeking to minister to Jesus' body, and in doing so they went on to become witnesses of the resurrection. Joseph, Nicodemus, Mary, Mary, Joanna and Salome were from very different social and religious backgrounds. Yet they were all followers of Jesus and came together in the difficult task of burying their friend. They were people whose faith was earthed.

The church continues as an organisation that has members at very different ends of the social scale. Worldwide, most Christians are poor and living in countries with a low GDP. Yet there are also Christians with powerful voices and it is important that they use their influence for good. In January 2015 Pope Francis spoke out on climate change when he visited the Philippines: 'I don't know if it is all [man's fault] but the majority is; for the most part, it is man who continuously slaps down nature.'[22] Rowan Williams, former archbishop of Canterbury, supported the school climate strikes in 2019 and demonstrated with Christian Climate Action and Extinction Rebellion outside St Paul's Cathedral in April 2019. In June 2020, a joint statement was issued from the present archbishop, Justin Welby, and many other church leaders:

The world is slow to respond to climate change, hanging on to an increasingly precarious and unjust economic system. It is predominantly black lives that are being impacted by drought, flooding, storms and sea level rise… In order to fight environmental injustice, we must also fight racial injustice.[23]

Across the world there are many unknown and unsung heroes and heroines seeking to tackle human poverty and environmental degradation. Whether they are responding to the impact of a typhoon in Asia, treating Ebola victims in West Africa, or supporting refugees and seeking racial justice worldwide, their work is an intensely physical engagement with the practical problems of the 21st century. The examples from Southern Africa and Kenya above show how integrated approaches are not only theologically more authentic in terms of resurrection faith but also highly effective. These examples show resurrection in action, as the new covenant gives us glimpses of the restored new creation. Restoration can come even in the midst of creation groaning.

ECO TIP Christians have been leaders in the Fairtrade movement, and Fairtrade coffee, tea and chocolate are now readily available in many shops. Significantly, the major brands now have Fairtrade lines. There are other areas of Fairtrade that have implications for both environment and human justice. Why not try to go Fairtrade in one new area this year? You may like to investigate Fairtrade clothing and jewellery. There are a number of suppliers and they also have sustainability policies.[24] If you prefer to stick to your favourite brands, why not write to them to see if they have a Fairtrade policy? You might also be interested to follow up Climate Stewards and perhaps offset your own energy use or that of your church.

Bible study: God's new-creation people

Read 2 Corinthians 5:14–20

This passage follows an explanation about the resurrection body that each faithful person can hope for in the future, and explains the implications of this for today. Verse 17 is interesting. The Greek literally means 'If someone is in Christ: new creation.' The 2011 New International Version translates it as 'If anyone is in Christ, the new creation has come'.

1 What does Paul mean by Christ's love, and why should it compel us (vv. 14–15)?
2 What does it mean to be new creation (v. 17)?
3 How can we be reconcilers in a world torn apart by inequality and environmental destruction?
4 How does being Christ's ambassadors gather together all these ideas? What then should we be doing?

Notes

1   'Glutted!' *Eat the Alpujarras blog*, 15 November 2013, **eatthealpujarras.blogspot.com/2013/11/glutted.html** (accessed 21 August 2020).

2   R. Gordon, 'Globalization reaches the Alpujarras... again', *War Times*, 1 August 2013, **happening-here.blogspot.com/2013/08/globalization-reaches-alpujarras-again.html** (accessed 21 August 2020).

3   F. Lawrence, 'Spain's salad growers are modern-day slaves, say charities', *The Guardian*, 7 February 2011, **theguardian.com/business/2011/feb/07/spain-salad-growers-slaves-charities** (accessed 21 August 2020).

4   F. Lawrence, 'A gap in perception on migrant workers in Spain', *The Guardian*, 8 March 2011, **theguardian.com/global-development/poverty-matters/2011/mar/08/spain-migrant-workers-agriculture-harsh-conditions** (accessed 21 August 2020).

5   H. Grant, '"No food, water, masks or gloves": migrant farm workers in Spain at crisis point' *The Guardian*, 1 May 2020, **theguardian.com/global-development/2020/may/01/no-food-water-masks-or-gloves-migrant-farm-workers-in-spain-at-crisis-point** (accessed 21 August 2020).

6   UN, *The Millennium Development Goals Report 2015*, **un.org/millenniumgoals/2015_MDG_Report/pdf/MDG%202015%20rev%20(July%201).pdf** (accessed 24 August 2020).

7   UN, 'Sustainable development', **sdgs.un.org** (accessed 24 August 2020).

8   UN, *The Sustainable Development Goals Report 2020*, **unstats.un.org/sdgs/report/2020/The-Sustainable-Development-Goals-Report-2020.pdf** (accessed 24 August 2020).

9   Bill and Melinda Gates Foundation, *Covid-19: A global perspective*, Goalkeepers Report, 2020.

10   K. Raworth, *Doughnut Economics*, Kindle edition (Random House, 2017).

11   Climate Stewards, **climatestewards.org** (accessed 3 July 2020).

12   The term 'global commons' is typically used to indicate the Earth's shared natural resources. See **en.wikipedia.org/wiki/Global_commons** (accessed 3 July 2020).

13 N.T. Wright, 'Christian origins and the resurrection of Jesus as a historical problem', *Sewanee Theological Review* 41 (1998), pp. 107–23.

14 A further expansion of these passages can be found in M.J. Hodson and M.R. Hodson, *Green Reflections* (BRF, 2021).

15 S. Durber, S. Richardson and B. Kikuyu, *Song of the Prophets: A global theology of climate change* (Christian Aid, 2020), **christianaid.org. uk/resources/about-us/song-prophets-global-theology-climate-change** (accessed 25 August 2020).

16 T. Makgoba, 'Hope and the environment: a perspective from the majority world', *Anvil* 29 (2013), pp. 55–70.

17 Research reports and details of other publications produced by the A Rocha Kenya conservation and science team can be found at www. **arocha.or.ke/work/scientific-research/marine** (accessed 3 July 2020).

18 R.D. Sluka and P. Simonin, 'Marine capture fisheries – a call to action in response to limits, unintended consequences, and ethics', *Perspectives on Science and Christian Faith* 66 (2014), pp. 203–12.

19 R.D. Sluka, 'The hidden things of God in the ocean', *Anglican EcoCare: Journal of EcoTheology* 2 (2016), pp. 41–50.

20 B. Cowburn, R. Sluka, J. Smith and M.O.S. Mohamed, 'Tourism, reef condition and visitor satisfaction in Watamu Marine National Park, Kenya', *Western Indian Ocean Journal of Marine Science* 12 (2013), pp. 57–70.

21 R.D. Sluka, *Hope for the Ocean: Marine biodiversity, poverty alleviation and blessing the nations* (Grove Booklets, 2012).

22 P. Pullella, 'Pope says climate change mostly man's fault', *Reuters*, 15 January 2015, **scientificamerican.com/article/pope-says-climate-change-mostly-man-s-fault1** (accessed 19 August 2020).

23 Anglican Communion Environmental Network, 'Environmental racism statement', **acen.anglicancommunion.org/ media/416007/200619-acen-environmental-racism-statement-updated-200624_en.pdf** (accessed 19 August 2020).

24 Fairtrade clothing can be found at **peopletree.co.uk** and **nomadsclothing.com**; Fairtrade jewellery can be found at **ingleandrhode.co.uk** (all accessed 19 August 2020).

10 A COVENANT OF HOPE

The People's Climate March 2014

On 20 and 21 September 2014 a coalition of organisations arranged climate change marches around the world just before world leaders were due to meet to discuss the issue at the UN in New York. The New York meeting was itself a step along the way to the COP21 meeting in Paris in December 2015, at which a global agreement on cutting carbon emissions was due to be signed. Preparations were made for six months before the People's Climate March. The biggest march was always going to be in New York itself (it was estimated at 310,000 people). In the week beforehand the then general secretary of the UN, Ban Ki-moon, announced that he would be on the New York march, and he was joined by Christiana Figueres, executive secretary of the UN Framework Convention on Climate Change (UNFCCC), Al Gore, former Vice-President of the USA, and actor Leonardo DiCaprio. In London, The Climate Coalition organised the biggest (approximately 40,000 people) of several marches in the UK, and those present included the actress Emma Thompson, the singer Peter Gabriel and Richard Chartres, the Bishop of London, who gave a powerful speech at the rally.

In September 2014 we were on our sabbatical trip in the Sierra Nevada, Spain. We decided to make every effort to go on a march. We checked on the web, expecting that the nearest march would involve a bus journey into Granada, but we had a surprise when we discovered a march in Portugos, a village just a short walk down the road from Pitres where we were staying. We rather expected that the numbers would be small, and set off on the Sunday wondering what we would find. When we got to Portugos it was not easy to find the march, and we did quite a lot of marching just to do so! But eventually we found a brave group of environmentalists bearing two posters saying '*Si el clima es muy fragil tambien tu $*' ('If the climate is very fragile, so are your dollars.') There were 13 of us and four dogs, so not quite on the scale of New York or London. We took photos of our march outside the town hall and then went to a bar for a drink and a chat.

There were thought to be 600,000 people on the marches worldwide, but did they have any impact? We are not sure, but they are a sign of hope. Two days later at the Climate Summit in New York, President Obama at least acknowledged the marches: 'So the climate is changing faster than our efforts to address it. The alarm bells keep ringing. Our citizens keep marching. We cannot pretend we do not hear them.'[1]

Climate strikes

Obama was right, and the citizens have kept marching. But it was probably not the ones he expected. I (Martin) use Twitter a lot. For me it is a useful research tool rather than something to play with. If you follow the right people and organisations, it is possible to find out a lot of useful information, sometimes a long way ahead of the crowd. In autumn 2018, I spotted something unusual. A young Swedish girl called Greta Thunberg seemed to be gathering quite a following with her weekly 'Fridays for Future' strikes. Greta started her strikes outside the Swedish parliament building on 20 August 2018. They soon grew to an international youth movement. I first saw a small strike of school children in Oxford in January 2019, and throughout that year there was a phenomenal growth in the movement. Greta became a celebrity and was invited to speak all over the world. She took two daring trans-Atlantic trips on yachts from Europe to the United States and back. Throughout 2019 and early 2020 there was a huge amount of activity. Greta's speeches were turned into a book.[2] In January 2019 at the World Economic Forum in Davos she ended her speech with:

Adults keep saying, 'We owe it to young people to give them hope.' But I don't want your hope. I don't want you to be hopeful. I want you to panic. I want you to feel the fear I feel every day, and then I want you to act. I want you to act as you would in a crisis. I want you to act as if our house is on fire. Because it is.

We know what Greta means; we desperately want people to take action, and there is a false hope that leads to complacency. But there is a place for real hope, not thrust on to young people, but to keep each of us going in what can be very disheartening times. And there is a place for Christian hope. In this final chapter we will look at some projects that inspire hope, and at what the Bible has to say about hope.

A small diversion

It is not every power plant that gets reviews on TripAdvisor®! We often use TripAdvisor® to check out hotels, restaurants and sites of interest when we are on our travels. While we were researching the topic of energy in Spain (chapter 6) we found that the solar energy plant at Sanlúcar la Mayor, west of Seville, actually had five reviews (in 2020 this was 19), mostly from green-energy types.[3] As we were travelling westwards from our mountain retreat in the Sierra Nevada to the Doñana area we realised that we were passing within a few miles of Sanlúcar, and decided to make a small diversion to see it. We looked at some satellite images before going and knew that the plant was to the north-west of the town. As the TripAdvisor® comments suggested, the best views were from the hill on the edge of the town. We could see several large towers surrounded by mirrors. We then headed down the hill to get some close-up photos of the towers.

Evidently this was not the usual type of solar power installation, so we wondered what was going on here. There are several installations on the site using different solar technologies. The first to open in 2007 was PS10.[4] This consists of a tower 115 metres tall, surrounded by

624 large movable mirrors. These focus the sun's rays on to the top of the tower, where there is a receiver and a turbine, which generates electricity. The nearby PS20 is of similar, but improved, design and opened in 2009. Then there are the large Solnova plants.[5] These have parabolic mirrors, which can be moved to collect the sun's radiation. The radiation is then focused on a tube containing special oil, in order to heat the oil to 400°C, and this in turn is used to create steam, which drives a turbine to produce electricity. When complete the complex should be able to supply electricity to 180,000 homes. It is one of the largest such installations in the world, and demonstrates that we have the technical ability to supply much of the world's electricity from renewable sources. We need to do this, and do it quickly.

A Rocha Portugal

There are hopeful signs of Christians responding to the environmental crisis, and A Rocha has been a key organisation for this. Towards the end of our sabbatical we had the opportunity to visit Cruzinha, the first A Rocha centre, on the Alvor Estuary in the Algarve in southern Portugal. We mentioned Cruzinha, founded by Peter and Miranda Harris, in chapter 1.[6] Martin first visited Cruzinha in 1993, when Peter and Miranda were still resident there, and we both visited again in 2005. This time we thought it would be appropriate to interview the current executive director, Marcial Felgueiras, and he graciously agreed.

When did you first come to Cruzinha and why?
I first visited Cruzinha in the context of a university Christian summer training week in 1987, during which Peter Harris, A Rocha's founder, was one of the main speakers.

What does your work as executive director involve?
Right now, and because the new centre directors are just learning the ropes, I am still a bit involved in the day-to-day operation of a field study centre, plus involvement with nature conservation matters elsewhere in the Algarve and

further away. My work includes team management, budget management and guaranteeing all the necessary conditions for the team to operate. Sometimes it includes the extra thrill of getting involved in some kind of environmental protection campaign. This might mean collecting evidence of environmental destruction, writing letters to the local authorities or coordinating conservation efforts with other environmental NGOs.

What has been the most difficult problem you have encountered at Cruzinha?

In Portugal any environmental NGO faces serious financial problems. A Rocha, being a Christian environmental organisation, receives less support from society than other similar organisations.7 But the most difficult problem is, in the midst of these daily concerns, when one loses the vision of what A Rocha is in God's grand plan. Without that, one loses the hope and the purpose, and one starts looking at the organisation from a different viewpoint than the one from which God looks at it. From there all sorts of problems, often difficult to resolve, can come up.

What aspect of your work has given you the most joy?

A lot, actually: the daily reminders, big and small, that God is in charge of all our world and all our needs and concerns; and the different people (volunteers, visitors, researchers) that we interact with and in whom we see God at work in many different ways, from accepting God's redemption to transforming their daily habits. We had big victories in an environmental court case, the first ever in Portugal in the 30 years since we have had environmental laws. But also small victories like local people starting to understand the importance of a responsible environmental life. They might start recycling or saving water and electricity. There would be a very big list of things that give me joy.

What are your hopes for the future?
At the A Rocha Portugal level, I think we can grow within the country, including more and more people in small groups, where Christians and non-Christians work side by side, sharing life, hopes and dreams. We can also work for a better personal and community life, in which the local environment thrives and with it the general well-being of each community.

For the world and on a short-to-medium timescale, my main hope is for the Christian church to awake to its environmental responsibility. This would mean a major society shift and would have a tremendous positive impact at different levels. Above all it would send a message that a new paradigm of society, based on hope and transformation, is possible. This will happen where community interests and well-being are included in personal decisions. What we managed to do under the fear of Covid-19 should be enough to demonstrate that it's possible to change. This time we should change because of hope and not because of fear.

In the longer term, my hope is in Christ, for a redeemed society living on a renewed Earth, where all the species live in harmony, fulfilling God's vision described in the book of Isaiah.

Biblical reflection: Grace and hope for our world

A theme that has run through this book has been hope for the ultimate renewal of creation, and restoration of the broken relationships between God, people and the rest of nature. This is promised through the unfolding covenant in the Bible. It climaxes in the person and work of Christ, who inaugurates the new creation. These truths are explained through the 'hymn of Christ' in Philippians 2:1–13. The apostle Paul wrote this passage to encourage the Christians in Philippi to imitate Christ. This small Christian community was experiencing suffering, and Paul was seeking to explain why and also to encourage a positive response.

Like other passages about Christ's cosmic role, this passage makes it clear that Christ is 'in very nature God' (2:6). Rather than begin with Christ's role in creation (as in John 1 and Colossians 1), Philippians focuses on the work of Christ through his birth, death and resurrection. Jesus' humility is emphasised through his willing 'divestment' of himself. The Greek word used is *kenosis*, meaning 'to empty'. Christ's self-emptying led to his birth, life and ultimately his death on the cross. Through that astonishing act of self-sacrifice, God poured out his grace on us.

The outcome for Christ was restoration: 'God exalted him to the highest place' (2:9). The outcome for the world was redemption and the establishment of Christ's ultimate rule: 'at the name of Jesus every knee should bow, in heaven and on earth and under the earth' (2:10). Paul is almost certainly referring to humans at this point, but passages such as Psalm 148 show that every part of creation will one day bow to Christ and praise him. We saw in chapter 2 that God created the cosmos for his glory. His glory finds fulfilment in the work of Christ.

Paul encourages the Christians in Philippi to live in the light of the wonderful truth of Christ's sacrifice for the world and eternal reign over it. He encourages them to live in harmony and true humility with one another, putting the needs of others above their own. He explains that this is the natural response to being united in Christ (2:1–2), and he encourages them that 'it is God who works in you to will and to act in order to fulfil his good purpose' (2:13). These suffering Christians could take heart from knowing that, despite their difficult situation, God was at work in and through them.

When we genuinely grasp the amazing grace of God, through all that Christ has done for us, we also bow our knees and find God at work in us for his good purposes. We saw in chapter 8 that our call is often to work out these vast cosmic truths in very ordinary ways as we connect with our local communities. How can we make visible our praise of Christ as we follow him together?

Foxearth

Andy Lester is head of conservation for A Rocha UK. Here Andy writes about one of their projects:

> Over the past few years, A Rocha UK has been working to develop a wetland nature reserve at Foxearth Meadows on the Essex/Suffolk border within the River Stour flood plain. Since purchasing the site, A Rocha has been working hard to make the reserve both amazing for wildlife (with a focus on dragonflies and damselflies), but also incredible for people. In 2019, for example, there were over 40 events with volunteers and a number of school and church visits aiming to inspire and equip local people on all aspects of faith and nature conservation.[8]

Mobilising churches: Eco Church

One of the most hopeful signs we have seen in recent years has been the incredibly rapid growth of the Eco Church scheme. Here Helen Stephens, A Rocha UK's church relations manager, gives us an update:

> There has been a step change in the church's engagement on environmental issues since the first publication of this book. A Rocha UK launched Eco Church[9] across England and Wales in January 2016 and now has almost 3,000 registered churches across multiple denominations.[10] Eco Church provides a framework for churches to engage with environmental issues and progress through awards from bronze and silver to gold. 1,000 awards have been made since launch, including twelve gold awards. To achieve an award, churches demonstrate caring for the Earth in five key aspects of church life: worship and teaching; buildings; land; community and global engagement; and lifestyle.
>
> While the awards help to measure progress and maintain momentum, they are not the end goal; rather, Eco Church is a

toolbox to help mobilise churches and Christians to care for the Earth as part of their everyday work and witness.

The diversity of awarded churches is growing regionally and by denomination and in terms of how churches are really grappling with the environmental issues of our time. St James' Piccadilly, a gold-awarded church with a grade 1 listed building, source all their electricity renewably, including producing some of their own from solar PV panels on the roof. They manage their small area of land for wildlife to flourish and have recently embarked on a 'spring wheat' community project, connecting city dwellers to food production.

Future hope brought near

Some years ago we were both involved in a research project on hope. This began as a personal collaboration with Ruth Valerio, then with A Rocha UK, and it was also supported by JRI and the Jerusalem Trust. It started because our hope felt under strain in the face of the severe environmental crisis and the inaction of world governments and others. We were struggling with proximate hope, which is the practical hope that humanity can and will meet the environmental challenges of this century. This hope had failed us and we found ourselves tending toward an eschatological or future hope that ultimately creation would be restored. Our missing link was to find a hope to sustain us today. What we discovered through the project was a lot of hope!

Our work was eventually published in the *Anvil* journal[11] and, for us, the missing link was a resilient hope. Resilient hope draws on future hope and sustains us to persevere, whatever the challenges. Romans 5:3 sums this up: 'suffering produces perseverance; perseverance, character; and character, hope'.[12] One of the *Anvil* papers was written by Archbishop Thabo Makgoba, who has experienced the impact of many of the environmental problems outlined in this book (see chapter 9).[13] He concluded that we need to live and speak hopefully: 'Behavioural science tells us that whenever a positive vision is central, it becomes the touchstone that shapes our words, actions and policy-making, and the magnet that draws us forward. If we always focus on problems, we lose sight of where we are going, and get dragged down.' Thabo encourages us to focus on the teaching of Paul in Philippians 4:8: 'whatever is true, whatever is honourable, whatever is just, whatever is pure, whatever is pleasing, whatever is commendable, if there is any excellence and if there is anything worthy of praise, think about these things' (NRSV).

Another *Anvil* author, Richard Bauckham, explored the links between faith, hope and love in 1 Corinthians 13:13.[14] He sees these as mutually engaging, as each is needed to support the others. Hope is the means by which Christians engage with the world, but it needs to be renewed as the world and its challenges change. Our modern society encourages us towards the completely unrealistic hope of continued growth, where tomorrow will be richer and better than today. Bauckham exposes the critical flaws in this approach, which has led us into our present environmental crisis. He explains that we need to disentangle ultimate and present hope and be modest and realistic about what we might hope for today. He concludes, 'We may need to be prepared for a lot of just keeping going, sticking it out, not giving up when it would be easy to. But faith, hope and love, working, of course, with all the resources of knowledge and expertise that we can muster, must also lead us into new visions of the possible even within a sorely damaged world.' We can see these principles at work in the following account from New Zealand.

Is there hope for New Zealand's devastated forests?

John Sibley was Martin's neighbour when they were in a hall of residence as undergraduates at Swansea University. He went on to become a biology teacher and eventually moved to New Zealand. John recently retired from teaching and spends some of his time volunteering on Tiritiri Matangi Island. He kindly wrote a short piece about this and the conservation problems of New Zealand:

Hope and faith always go hand in hand. Whenever faith is strong, hope is sure, and this spurs us on to attempt great things in seemingly impossible situations. This is as true in the spiritual realms of life as in the material.

The impact of humans on the wildlife of New Zealand has been devastating. Geographical isolation with few predators has, over time, produced large, flightless birds and insects which are easy targets for exotic predators. The ancient forests remained little changed until the arrival of humans, but the influence of their colonisation has been profound. For 700 years humans have used fire to clear the forests for food production, and today less than 25 per cent of the original forest remains.[15] Over 53 mammal species, including voracious rats, stoats and possums were introduced.[16] New Zealand's large flightless birds were easy prey and showed little fear of newly introduced mammals. Today more than 40 per cent of New Zealand's native birds are extinct, with a further 30 per cent endangered. Some international ecologists declare New Zealand to be the most environmentally devastated nation on Earth. Nearly 2,000 exotic (many extremely invasive) weed and tree species have permanently changed the remaining native beech and podocarp forests. Although it is now thought that many species can exist alongside native species without taking over or rendering the environment unsuitable for native birdlife, other weeds are more pernicious (see chapter 2).

Hope exists in the form of almost 200 offshore islands, some acting as predator-free sanctuaries where endangered species can be translocated and numbers allowed to recover. Effective scientific conservation techniques and pest control strategies have been trialled and perfected in New Zealand over the past 30 years, and know-how is frequently exported to other countries experiencing similar problems. Education is vital, and the New Zealand school curriculum requires children to have knowledge of the environmental woes of the past and action for the future.

Island reserves such as Tiritiri Matangi,[17] 20 km north of

Auckland, are a good example of this sort of hope in action. Cleared of native forest for farming about 100 years ago, in the 1970s it was declared a recreational reserve and in the 1980s volunteers replanted 280,000 native saplings. Threatened bird species,[18] such as the takahe, stitchbird, kokako and saddleback, have been reintroduced and numbers have increased, enabling translocations to be made to other predator-free islands.

During this time Tiri has become an international model for restorative conservation techniques. As one of the educators working on Tiri Island, I lead parties of schoolchildren, university undergraduates and other visitors through the now bird-filled reforested tracks, explaining the problems of past and present times and the work done to remedy them. A careful balance has to be struck here, as it would be all too easy to leave students feeling fearful, despondent and powerless in the face of the myriad problems accumulated over the years.[19] We want our students and international visitors to be change agents in their future individual spheres of influence. Many of the world's environmental problems do have workable solutions, and if they leave Tiri Island hopeful and enthusiastic for change, we will have done our jobs well.

Grace and hope for the onward journey

Our sabbatical came to an end as the October sun began to change the seasons. Our journey back through Portugal and Spain took us overnight to Merida, a Roman city in the far west. The Roman buildings were amazing and we dashed around to see as much as possible before we moved on. There was a full amphitheatre and a beautiful theatre and garden, a bridge, a viaduct and much more. There were Visigoth archaeological remains, Moorish fortifications and a medieval city. As we looked around the Roman theatre, we were struck by how fragile this huge and strong empire was in the end. The emperors and the people must have once seen it as endless, and yet now all that is left are stones. The passing of empires was a reminder to us that our own culture is no more permanent and could also fail if we don't adapt and change to meet new conditions.

At last we reached Bilbao and soon found ourselves on the ferry back to Britain. We had much to think about from our weeks away. We had no doubt that the global situation is very serious indeed, but all is not lost. We have discovered that the beginning of real hope is the surrendering of unrealistic hope. The beginning of hope is to have a positive realism about what can be achieved. We won't bring back the ecological environments that have been damaged beyond repair; or the soils that have been lost; or the ancient aquifers that have been despoiled. We will not be able to hold back some climate change, and we are now committed to considerable changes in this century and beyond. We will not be able to entirely prevent these changes having a disproportionate impact on the poorest people in the world. As Christians, what we can do is care for the wider world in practical ways and seek justice for both people and planet. We can work to mitigate and prevent environmental damage, and we can support our local communities in looking after the environment. We do this strengthened through the hope that rests on the security we have in Christ and his commitment to our world. In Colossians 1:15–20, Christ is described as holding creation, and the Church is described as his body. Christ invites us into a covenant partnership to hold our suffering world with him and be a means of his grace in helping it toward a more sustainable future. In going forward we will find ourselves alongside many others: Christians, secular people and those of other faiths. We have reached a crucial moment in history and Christ calls us to be his disciples in a world struggling with environmental crisis. As we do, we will find covenant hope to take us forward.

Epilogue, January 2021

Having written the first edition of this book on sabbatical in Spain, we worked on the second edition as summer 2020 drew to a close. We look back on that eventful summer with terrific sadness for the pain and bereavement that so many suffered and are still suffering around the world. We have seen inequalities exposed and political and economic structures shaken, with not all surviving. We cannot predict what the future will hold. We do not yet know the result of the 26th UN Climate Change Conference of the Parties (COP26) in November 2021. We don't yet know the long-term impacts of the Covid-19 pandemic.

We continue to hold on to our covenant hope in Christ as we seek to play our small part in building a just and sustainable world. We are strengthened by words from Hebrews 6:19: 'We have this hope as an anchor for the soul, firm and secure.' May you also find that hope and may God lead you onward in faith.

ECO TIP Your church may be at the stage of pursuing a green scheme such as Eco Church, and that's brilliant! If it is not quite at that point, one very positive thing would be to hold a special 'eco-evening'. Invite some friends round and share a bit about your thinking on the Christian faith, God's creation and how this works together with caring for the most vulnerable people in the world. Even if just a few people came, it would mean a few more now thinking about these things. Remember that mighty oaks grow from small acorns!

Bible study: kingdom faith – growing seeds and calming a storm

In Mark 4:26–41 there are two parables and one miracle that teach about faith and Christ's relationship with creation.

Read Mark 4:26–29

1 What is Jesus saying about our understanding of nature?
2 What does this say about Jesus' view of how we should interact with nature – should we just leave it alone?
3 How can we improve our 'environmental harvest'? In what way would this reveal the kingdom of God?

Read Mark 4:30–34

One of our much loved home churches is Christ Church, Jerusalem, where Martin became a Christian. In the courtyard there is a large mustard tree. It is a mustard tree that Jesus is referring to, not the small herb sometimes grown with cress.

4 What smaller actions might you take to help sustain our struggling Earth?
5 How could these ideas grow within your own church community and beyond?

Read Mark 4:35–41

6 What does this story tell us about Jesus' relationship with nature?
7 What hope does it give us in a time of environmental crisis?
8 In what ways can we demonstrate this message of hope to those around us?
9 Do we need to be practical?

You might like to end your study with a time of prayer.

Notes

1   T. Randall, 'Obama to UN: "The alarm bells keep ringing, our citizens keep marching"', *Bloomberg*, 23 September 2014, **bloomberg.com/ news/articles/2014-09-23/obama-to-un-the-alarm-bells-keep- ringing-our-citizens-keep-marching-** (accessed 24 August 2020).

2   G. Thunberg, *No One Is Too Small to Make a Difference* (Penguin Books, 2019).

3   TripAdvisor®, 'Solar power plants', *Things to do in Sanlúcar la Mayor*, **tripadvisor.co.uk/Attraction_Review-g776222-d2355463-Reviews- Solnova_Solar_Power_Station-Sanlucar_la_Mayor_Province_of_ Seville_Andalucia.html** (accessed 24 August 2020).

4   'First EU commercial concentrating solar power tower opens in Spain', *Alternative Energy Info*, 31 March 2007, **ens-newswire.com/ ens/mar2007/2007-03-30-02.asp** (accessed 24 August 2020).

5   PowerTechnology, 'Solar Tower, Seville', **power-technology.com/ projects/seville-solar-tower** (accessed 12 January 2021).

6   P. Harris, *Under the Bright Wings* (Regent College, 2000).

7   A Rocha Portugal, **arocha.pt/en** (accessed 17 July 2020).

8   A Rocha, 'The marvel of Foxearth Meadows', **arocha.org.uk/ our-activities/practical-conservation/foxearth-meadows/ the-marvel-of-foxearth-meadows** (accessed 10 July 2020).

9   Eco Church, **ecochurch.arocha.org.uk** (accessed 28 August 2020).

10 Eco Congregation is a similar scheme operating in Scotland, Ireland and other countries. See **ecocongregation.org** (accessed 28 August 2020).

11 The papers on environment and hope in *Anvil* can be downloaded free from **jri.org.uk/publications/environment-and-hope** (accessed 25 September 2020).

12 M.R. Hodson, 'Discovering a robust hope for life on a fragile planet', *Anvil* 29 (2013), pp. 1–6.

13 T. Makgoba, 'Hope and the environment: a perspective from the majority world', *Anvil* 29 (2013), pp. 55–70.

14 R. Bauckham, 'Ecological hope in crisis?' *Anvil* 29 (2013), pp. 43–54.

15 'Deforestation in New Zealand', Wikipedia, **en.wikipedia.org/wiki/ Deforestation_in_New_Zealand** (accessed 12 January 2021).

16 Department of Conservation, 'Pests and threats', **doc.govt.nz/ nature/pests-and-threats** (accessed 30 May 2020).

17 Tiritiri Matangi Open Sanctuary, **tiritirimatangi.org.nz** (accessed 30 May 2020).

18 Department of Conservation, 'Birds A–Z', **doc.govt.nz/nature/native-animals/birds/birds-a-z** (accessed 30 May 2020).

19 D. Liverman, 'How to teach about climate without making your students feel hopeless.' *The Washington Post*, 20 August 2014, **washingtonpost.com/posteverything/wp/2014/08/20/how-to-teach-about-climate-without-making-your-students-feel-hopeless** (accessed 30 May 2020).

BIBLE STUDY LEADER'S NOTES

Chapter 1: the greatest commandment

Matthew 22:34-40

Jesus puts loving God as the foremost of the commandments. This should be the core of everything we do. But the second commandment can be derived from it: we cannot love God and not love our neighbour, whom God created and loves. Much of Jesus' teaching, especially in the Sermon on the Mount (Matthew 5-7), is an expansion of this summary. There are also Old Testament examples of how not to behave, such as Jonah, who lacked the compassion that God had for the Ninevites. In our churches we will not go wrong if we focus on these two commandments as our key aims. Both commandments are a challenge as we consider the current environmental crisis. Can we truly say we love God if we treat his world so badly? Do we really love our neighbour if our actions leave them with a highly degraded world to live in? What about future generations? How do we love them as ourselves?

Luke 10:25-37

We can consider these ideas further through the parable of the good Samaritan. Many species in the world are threatened by human activity. It is a natural extension of this parable to consider them alongside humans who are suffering because of environmental destruction. Both need our help and support, and we cannot effectively help one without helping the other. As we look at Jesus' commands afresh we can find a new challenge for our love, and a fresh approach to loving God and caring for our world.

Chapter 2: creation in God's commandments

Exodus 20:1–17

1 God is engaged with his creation: he acts within it to rescue Israel, as well as bringing judgement and covenant love. God is distinct from his creation – he forbids the making of idols. God does not want us to worship his creation.
2 God longs for us to be in a loving relationship with him. This is sustained by keeping his commandments, by worshipping him and by maintaining respectful relationships. Jesus summed this up in his greatest commandment (Matthew 22:34–40).
3 Sabbath is about both rest and respect. All creation needs rest and we show respect for God's world when we not only rest ourselves but give rest to other people and to the world's biodiversity. God has given us leadership over creation (Genesis 1:28) and we should take this responsibility seriously.
4 This commandment to observe the sabbath rest was very radical – slaves and domestic animals were rarely given rest in the ancient world. This shows how God values all that he has made.
5 Do we really keep the ten commandments if we live our lives in a way that honours God and honours our neighbour, but does not honour the creation that God made and values? God commands us not to murder, despoil, steal, deceive or covet, yet so often we have used the natural world for our own ends and one or more of these words could apply to our actions.

You may like to end your Bible study with a time of prayer for the natural world immediately around you, and for parts of the world where biodiversity is under pressure. You could read Psalm 104 as a conclusion to your time together.

Chapter 3: living lives that declare the glory of God

Psalm 19

1 The first part of this Psalm is focused on the glories of the heavens but all of nature declares God's glory and you may like to share widely on what you value in the natural world.
2 We instinctively give thanks to God when we see his handiwork!
3 We have overused natural resources to such an extent that they have not been able to renew themselves and this has left many places in the world damaged and degraded.
4 We have simply not realised the impact of many of our life choices on the natural world. When fossil fuels started to be used, no one realised the impact on climate. Now we do know and we need to make a change.
5 There are many answers to this! Our consumer society 'rules over us' and the culture of our fast-moving world. The shock of lockdown in 2020 might have opened eyes to a slower paced life and a simpler lifestyle.

It is important to bring our focus back to our wonderful God and to trust him to be our Rock and our Redeemer. The world is in a difficult place but he is our strength.

Chapter 4: salvation for people and creation

Isaiah 55:6–13

1 The landscape described in the book of Isaiah is that of ancient Canaan. It would have been typical of many Mediterranean countries, and you may like to draw on holiday experiences in imagining it. Isaiah describes farmed hills and valleys with some woodland and some wilder areas, both arid and mountainous. Local people depended on rains in season for their crops and were vulnerable if these rains failed.

2 British people are great at talking about the weather! But do we value our climate? Recent floods and droughts have caused some communities to think differently about the value of rain. God has a purpose for his word. As the rain waters the ground and brings forth fruit, so God longs for his word to produce fruit in our lives. It is as we 'seek the Lord' (v. 5) that we are enriched through his word. This points us towards the salvation he offers us.

3 Jesus described himself as the 'bread of life' (John 6:35) and the 'true vine' (John 15:1). He used natural images for people who lived close to the soil. In establishing Communion with bread and wine he was also pointing towards the future hope of a restored creation, where all will flourish. There is therefore a glimpse of salvation for all creation (see Bible study in Chapter 8).

4 Taking part in a fellowship meal of reconciliation involved a commitment to work together for the present and future good of both parties. As we take the fruit of the Earth to remember our own salvation in Christ, we might also like to make a commitment to care for the Earth entrusted to us. Your church could decide on a practical action to go alongside a Communion service.

5 This may take quite a bit of discussion. One thought would be to look at songs and any liturgy that you use in church. Do they remind you of creation and, if not, could you make any changes? You may like to give thanks consciously for creation, both for its beauty and for all that it gives us.[1]

Chapter 5: making life-giving choices

1 Peter 4:1–11

The list of sins in this passage is not exactly encouraging! By discussing the drivers of consumption at the beginning of the session you may help people to connect with the passage and take a fresh look at the shortcomings of their own lives. Question 1 could stray on to a discussion of predestination versus free will. You may like to limit this if it starts to dominate the study! The passage is a challenging one and you may wish to take time in prayer at the end. With lifestyle changes it is important to make a series of smaller changes that stick rather than larger ones that fade out.

Chapter 6: sabbath, new wine and fresh approaches

Luke 5:33–39; 6:1–10

Many of Jesus' followers were from relatively non-religious backgrounds. In using the image of the bridegroom at the banquet, Jesus was expressing his joy at his new followers. Jesus used the new cloth and new wine images to explain why his disciples needed to have more flexible approaches. There is much to be discussed from the perspective of Christian discipleship. We can also use these principles to reimagine our lives as we seek to come out of a high-energy-use lifestyle.

In the second passage from Luke 6, Jesus expresses views that would have been current among the more open of the Pharisees but were not popular with those who were stricter. The main point is that the sabbath should be life-giving to all.

Chapter 7: soil, figs and vineyards

Isaiah 5:1–7; Luke 13:6–9

Both these parables are referring to God's people, who are very far from where God would want them to be. Isaiah declared that Israel was under judgement and was about to be taken into exile. In the passage from Luke, there is the potential of judgement, but one more chance to respond. These parables were written for a general rather than an environmental context, but there are good potential applications to our need to respond to our damage of the environment today. We have one final chance to truly hold back the damage we are doing to our planet.

Chapter 8: loaves, fishes and the bread of life

John 6:1–15

1 This is a very familiar story and the question is intended to draw on people's previous responses to it.
2 Jesus performs a miracle of abundance. This affirms his role as the agent of creation and also gives a glimpse of new creation.
3 Let people discuss this. Many caring motives are expressed.

John 6:30–40

4 Moses was from God and God provided manna to the Israelites in the wilderness. Jesus made a miraculous picnic. People were connecting the two events and wondering who Jesus was. Jesus links manna with his incarnation.
5 Jesus uses the staple food to give a glimpse into the reality of eternal life.
6 Jesus ends by promising resurrection. You may like to discuss how this connects with the bread of life (see Bible study in Chapter 4).

Chapter 9: God's new-creation people

2 Corinthians 5:14–20

1 Paul is explaining that Jesus' love was so great that he was willing to die for us (John 3:16). We will also die but we will see resurrection. Therefore we should live for Christ.
2 The implication of this verse is that, when we turn to Christ and are redeemed, we in some way become new creation.
3 This needs us to understand the interconnectedness of human and environmental problems, as well as poverty, disease and conflict.
4 It is part of our basic calling as Christians to engage with these issues and seek reconciliation. We have the awesome responsibility to bring new creation.

Chapter 10: Kingdom faith: growing seeds and calming a storm

Mark 4:26–34

1   Today we know far more about the workings of nature than people in Jesus' day but we still do not have full knowledge of it. We need to respect nature.
2   Jesus often uses farming illustrations and this is an encouragement for us to engage with nature.
3–5 Christians often find it hard to link their environmental concern with their faith, and yet positive actions for the environment are gospel actions.

Mark 4:35–41

6–9 This passage reveals Christ as Lord of creation (John 1:1–5; Colossians 1:15–20), and gives us hope that he is holding on to creation and has the power to act as we intercede for it. We demonstrate this to those around us when we show our commitment to caring for God's Earth in practical and other ways.

Note

1   You can find some further discussion on Isaiah 55:6–13 in M.R. Hodson, 'Creative harmony: Isaiah's vision of a sustainable future' in R.J. Berry (ed.), *When Enough is Enough: A Christian framework for environmental sustainability* (IVP, 2007), pp. 167–77.

BIBLIOGRAPHY

R. Bauckham, *Bible and Ecology: Rediscovering the community of creation* (DLT, 2010).

C. Bell and R.S. White, *Creation Care and the Gospel: Reconsidering the mission of the church* (Hendrickson, 2016).

D. Bookless, *Planetwise: Dare to care for God's world* (IVP, 2008).

P. Harris, *Under the Bright Wings* (Regent College Publishing, 1993).

P. Harris, *Kingfisher's Fire: A story of hope for God's Earth* (Monarch, 2008).

K. Hayhoe and A. Farley, *A Climate for Change: Global warming facts for faith-based decisions* (FaithWords, 2009).

M.J. Hodson and M.R. Hodson, *Cherishing the Earth: How to care for God's creation* (Monarch, 2008).

M.R. Hodson and M.J. Hodson (eds) Environment and Hope edition of *Anvil*. The whole 2013 journal is available to be downloaded at **jri.org.uk/publications/environment-and-hope**.

M.J. Hodson and M.R. Hodson, *An Introduction to Environmental Ethics* (Grove Books, Cambridge, 2017).

M.J. Hodson and M.R. Hodson, *Green Reflections: Biblical inspiration for sustainable living* (BRF, 2021).

J.T. Houghton, *Global Warming: The complete briefing*, fifth edition (Cambridge University Press, 2015).

M. Maslin, *Climate Change: A very short introduction*, third edition (Oxford University Press, 2014).

R. Valerio, *Just Living: Faith and community in an age of consumerism* (Hodder & Stoughton, 2017).

R. Valerio, *'L' is for Lifestyle: Christian living that doesn't cost the Earth* revised and updated edition (IVP, 2019).

R. Valerio, *Saying Yes to Life* (SPCK, 2019).

R. Valerio, M.J. Hodson, M.R. Hodson and T. Howles, *Covid-19: Environment, justice, and the future* (Grove, 2020).

USEFUL WEBSITES

A Rocha, Christians in Conservation, is an international organisation with centres in many countries. Examples of their work can be found in many chapters of this book. **arocha.org/en**

The Anglican Alliance brings together those in the Anglican family of churches and agencies to work for a world free of poverty and injustice. **anglicanalliance.org**

Anglican Communion Environmental Network (ACEN) aims to encourage Anglicans to support sustainable environmental practices as individuals and in the life of their communities. **acen.anglicancommunion.org**

Au Sable Institute of Environmental Studies was founded in 1980 in the United States. It inspires and educates people to serve, protect and restore God's Earth. Au Sable offers environmental science programmes for students and adults of all ages: primary and secondary school, college and graduate school. **ausable.org**

Christian Aid is an agency of the churches in the UK and Ireland that has a vision to end poverty. **christianaid.org.uk**

Christian Rural and Environmental Studies (CRES) runs certificate and diploma courses by distance learning. CRES is run jointly by The John Ray Initiative and A Rocha UK, and is validated by Ripon College, Cuddesdon, near Oxford. Martin Hodson is principal tutor for CRES. **cres.org.uk**

Climate Stewards is a carbon offsetting initiative that is part of the A Rocha network (see chapters 6 and 9). **climatestewards.org**

The Churches Together in Britain and Ireland (CTBI) Environmental Issues Network (EIN) is a network that seeks to coordinate all the various Christian networks, organisations and denominations with a focus on the environment. Their webpage gives a comprehensive list of these organisations in the UK and there are also links to joint campaigns and initiatives. **ctbi.org.uk/ environment-churches-and-christian-organisations**

Eco Church is an ecumenical programme in England and Wales helping churches to make the link between environmental issues and Christian faith, and to respond with practical action in the church, in the lives of individuals, and in the local and global community. The programme is administered by A Rocha UK (see chapter 10). **ecochurch.arocha.org.uk**

European Christian Environmental Network is the main working instrument of the Conference of European Churches for addressing the need for environmental engagement and response to climate change. **ecen.org**

Evangelical Environmental Network (EEN) from North America is a ministry dedicated to the care of God's creation. EEN seeks to equip, inspire, disciple and mobilise God's people in their efforts to care for God's creation. **creationcare.org**

The Faraday Institute for Science and Religion is an interdisciplinary research enterprise based at St Edmund's College, Cambridge. **faraday.cam.ac.uk**

The Farming Community Network (FCN) seeks to provide confidential, non-judgemental support to all those in need of help in the farming community, whether the issue is related to the farm business or the farm household (see chapter 4). **fcn.org.uk**

Green Christian is an interdenominational UK Christian organisation for people concerned about the environment. **greenchristian.org.uk**

The John Ray Initiative (JRI) aims to bring together Christian and scientific understanding of the environment. Martin Hodson is operations director for JRI, and examples of their work can be found in several chapters of this book. **jri.org.uk**

The Lausanne Movement connects influencers and ideas for global mission and has networks for a number of global issues. The network for Creation Care promotes stewardship of God's creation as a biblical command and an integral part of what it means to follow Jesus. **lausanne.org/networks/issues/creation-care**

Operation Noah is an ecumenical Christian charity in the UK providing leadership, focus and inspiration in response to the growing threat of catastrophic climate change. **operationnoah.org**

Tearfund is an international Christian development agency that is passionate about ending poverty. **tearfund.org**

Care for creation with A Rocha UK

A Rocha UK's mission is to mobilise Christians and churches in the UK to care for the environment as a normal part of their discipleship. We are fulfilling this mission through our key programmes: Wild Christian, our conservation network, Partners in Action, which includes our own nature reserves, Eco Church and convening to reach Christians, Christian land managers, church and church leaders with a creation care message on a national scale.

Our work doesn't stop there. A Rocha UK is part of a worldwide family of A Rocha organisations, serving with others who share a passion for the planet.

If you would like to hear more from us, please visit **arocha.org.uk/join-us**, email **uk@arocha.org** or phone 020 8574 5935. You can also follow us on social media on Twitter **@ARochaUK**, on Instagram **@arocha_uk** and on Facebook **@A Rocha UK.**

Christian Rural and Environmental Studies

CRES offers a unique opportunity to study the latest developments in environmental and rural studies from a Christian perspective. The two-year certificate course and two-year diploma are distance-learning courses validated by Ripon College Cuddesdon (RCC). CRES is jointly run by The John Ray Initiative and A Rocha UK. Students are assigned to local tutors and invited to study days and an annual conference at RCC.

Students take six of the twelve modules and write a dissertation on a topic of their own choosing. The diploma involves an extended research project, and this course is usually taken by those who have already completed the certificate. CRES welcomes applications from beyond the UK. There are no entry requirements. The cost in 2021 is £900 in total, which includes two residential weekends and four day conferences, payable in two annual instalments.

Principal tutor: Dr Martin J. Hodson

Email: **cres@jri.org.uk**; *website:* **cres.org.uk**

The John Ray Initiative (JRI)

The John Ray Initiative (JRI) is an educational charity, founded in 1998, with a vision to bring together scientific and Christian understandings of the environment in a way that can be widely communicated and lead to effective action. JRI's mission is to promote responsible environmental stewardship in accordance with Christian principles and the wise use of science and technology. Inspiration for JRI is taken from John Ray (1627–1705), English naturalist, Christian theologian and first biological systematist of modern times, preceding Carl Linnaeus.

JRI has a specific education focus, concentrating on conferences, courses and publications. In-house publications are mainly *Briefing Papers* on a wide variety of subjects which connect the environment, science and Christianity. These are available as downloads from the JRI website, which is also the home of *The JRI Blog* with frequent posts from a number of contributors. JRI staff and associates also publish books, papers, articles and blog posts for many other publishers and organisations. With an ever-increasing focus on electronic communication, JRI runs an email list with monthly mailings to inform about its own activities and about events that may be of interest. It is also active on social media, connecting to current conversations and giving a Christian voice to environmental concerns.

Sign up for our monthly and local emails at **jri.org.uk.** Join the conversation on Facebook **JohnRayInitiative** and Twitter **@JRayI**; contact us at **admin@jri.org.uk**

INDEX OF BIBLE VERSES

TOPICAL INDEX

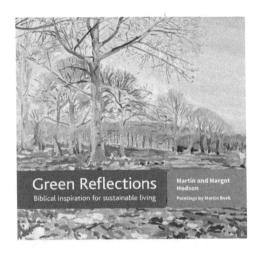

How should we look after the world we inhabit? Martin and Margot Hodson bring together scientific and theological wisdom to offer 62 reflections inspired by the Bible. Encouraging both contemplation and response, these thoughtful explorations include themes such as the wisdom of trees, landscapes of promise and sharing resources.

Green Reflections
Biblical inspiration for sustainable living
Martin J. Hodson and Margot R. Hodson
Paintings by Martin Beek
978 1 80039 068 3 £8.99

brfonline.org.uk

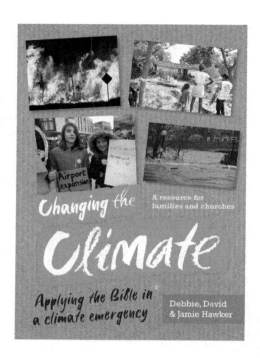

Changing the Climate unpacks a series of Bible passages to show the Bible's relevance to environmentalism, and how we can all play our part in limiting the negative effects of climate change. This workbook can be used by families, youth groups, church study groups and individuals. Each of the twelve chapters looks at a particular Bible passage, connects it with climate action, poses questions, suggests practical steps that can be taken and provides stories from around the world.

Changing the Climate
Applying the Bible in a climate emergency
Debbie, David and Jamie Hawker
978 1 80039 022 5 £9.99

brfonline.org.uk

CPSIA information can be obtained
at www.ICGtesting.com
Printed in the USA
BVHW090918070521
606655BV00007B/993